Children of the Flesh,
Children of the Promise

Children of
the Flesh,

Children of
the Promise

A RABBI TALKS WITH PAUL

Jacob Neusner

THE PILGRIM PRESS
CLEVELAND, OHIO

The Pilgrim Press, Cleveland, Ohio 44115

00 99 98 97 96 95   5 4 3 2 1

Library of Congress Cataloging-in-Publication Data

Neusner, Jacob, 1932–
    Children of the flesh, children of the promise : a rabbi talks
with Paul / Jacob Neusner.
        p.   cm.
    Includes bibliographical references and index.
    ISBN 0-8298-1026-9
    1. Judaism—Apologetic works. 2. Jews—Identity. 3. Paul, the
Apostle, Saint—Views on Judaism. 4. Rabbinical literature—History
and criticism. 5. Christianity—Controversial literature.
    I. Title.
    BM648.N43   1995
    296.3—dc20   94-43176
                                                            CIP

Contents

Preface

THIS BOOK SETS FORTH a debate between myself and the apostle Paul as well as a principal contemporary spokesperson for Paul's view that Israel is an ethnic entity within the framework of a Judaic system.[1] I will show that the Judaism that has set the norms from nearly the time of Paul to our own day conceives of its Israel as never ethnic, but solely transcendental. The Judaism of the dual Torah[2] cannot make the distinction critical to Paul's thought about Israel— the distinction between children of the flesh and children of the promise. To be a child of the promise for Judaism is to be a child, also, of the flesh, and vice versa.

Because Christianity (through Paul) and Judaism (through my representation of its authoritative sources) concur that Israel is the bearer of God's blessing, the issue of the ethnicity of Israel proves critical: who stands for God in the world? Is it a transcendental community, framed by the revealed Torah of Sinai and governed by the terms of that covenant? That is the view of the Judaism we will consider here. Or is it a this-worldly community, bearing in its midst also a component of those who identify themselves through faith (in Jesus Christ) and joined, too, by outsiders to its ethnic framework, also identified through that same faith, also part of those children of the promise? If Israel is a wholly supernatural community, as Judaism maintains, then the ethnic definition falls away. If Israel is ethnic but may also form a community of salvation, then the ethnic definition takes a critical place in the account of who, and what, Israel is.

The conversation between myself and Paul is constructed out of three readings of Israel paramount in the Torah as set forth by the sages: Israel is unique or sui generis; Israel is defined by genealogy; Israel is the elect of God, the chosen people. All three readings carry conviction for Paul's and Christianity's formulation of Israel; all on the surface appear ethnic—indeed, religious formulations of ethnic self-celebration. But by those categories, sages meant something in no way narrow or ethnic or self-celebratory. The conversation gets under way when we pay attention to what the Judaic sages meant when they spoke of unique, holy, genealogical, and national Israel, as they do on every page of their voluminous writings.

What difference does the outcome of this conversation make? The conviction of this book is that what the world needs least is one more ethnic religion. What humanity most requires is to make real that vision, set forth by every universal religion, of a single race of men and women. The issue is whether or not Judaism is ethnic and particular or universal and general in its categories and perspectives and vision. At stake is the role Judaism is going to take in the next century's world order.

Will a narrow, inward-facing, closed ethnic religion predominate? Then the next century's diaspora Judaism—self-absorbed and narrowing the sympathies of the faithful to their own self-esteem—will prove disruptive and ethnic. It will be the religion of those rabbis of Jerusalem who, in 1993, boycotted a world conference held in Jerusalem by preeminent religious leaders—Catholic cardinals, Lutheran bishops, and many others—and announced, "They have nothing to say to us, and we have nothing to say to them!" That formulation of matters in the name of the God of a single nation fully embodies the ethnic religion that our sages despised and rejected in the Mishnah, Midrash compilations, and two Talmuds: the religion of Israel's God who is not also the God of all humanity, the religion produced by anti-Semitic caricatures of Judaism and that the Israeli rabbinate, in its isolation and ignorance, endorses.

Or will Judaism conceive its vision out of a perspective of Israel that forms a source of concern and commitment to the service of one God for all humanity? Then that Judaism—which I claim is the Judaic vision of the framers of the faith, comparable in its universal aspiration to the Christian vision of Jesus and Paul—will serve as a source of blessing to humanity. The difference is the character of the vision. I will show through analogies drawn from Christianity that the Judaism set forth by the sages of the written and oral Torah is one-sidedly universal in its categories, in its vision, in its aspiration to be and to serve.

Then, it follows, the context for discussion is a dialogue with two parties: first, Judaism's companion through history, Christianity, which regards as established the view that Judaism is an ethnic religion; and, second, the diaspora—those Jews living outside of the state of Israel—who are sure that while there may or may not be a God, the Jewish people are certainly God's chosen people in a tangible and this-worldly sense. The setting of the dialogue is a single social setting, the United States, with its unique conception of the interplay of ethnic identification, nationality, citizenship, and the rights and responsibilities of all persons, differentiated not by origin or race or station in society but by character and conscience, expressed in deed.

Islam and Christianity exemplify universal religions, deeply particular to various nations and peoples, yet possessed of a transforming vision of humanity under God's rule, in God's image. For the purpose of this book, Christianity will form the model of a universal religion; its view of Judaism will be the goad and the challenge. Christianity regards itself as universal and its competition, Judaism, as particular. I will show that this view contradicts the doctrines of the Judaism that defines the norms. This Judaism deals in a particular way with the particularity of the group, forming out of what is an ethnic identification a religious identity that encompasses Jew and Greek, man and woman, free and slave alike. Judaism, in its classical form in antiquity, is a religion of broad, human vision. What Christianity asks of Jesus Christ, this Judaism asks of its Israel, its conception of Israel serving in some of the critical ways in which Christ serves within Christianity. The Judaism to which I refer is not "the religion of the Old Testament" that people wrongly assume stands for Judaism, but the Judaism of the dual Torah.

Israel[3] in Judaism, like Church or mystical body of Christ in Christianity, forms a metaphor (drawing upon the here and now of the realized community) for how God works out the contradictions of the human condition: Adam contrasts then with Israel, just as the first Adam contrasts with Christ, the last Adam. And when we speak of Adam, that is, of humanity, the ethnic gives way to a conception that is universal and all-encompassing.

This book therefore concerns how we conceive that God relates to us. It is not a book about the religious politics of ethnicity—God loves our club more than yours—but about how we know whether a religion is ethnic and why it matters. Let me frame the questions very simply. Do we (meaning our particular ethnic group) make God our own, to the exclusion of others and the aggrandizement of ourselves? Or is religion a medium for the nurture of a shared sense of humanity among all peoples?

The issue here is religion and God, not the effects of religion upon the politics of the social order. So what is at stake, to take a current example, is not the German citizenship law, which makes slight provision for territorially, linguistically, and culturally defined Germans of Turkish origin and Islamic faith, even those of the third generation in Berlin or Frankfurt. For this is not at all a book about political problems. The political crisis brought on by Germany's difficulty in dealing with third-generation German-born Turks serves only to underscore what is at stake in the conception of an ethnic religion: religion as a force of exclusion or inclusion.

And that is only an example of what I take to be a nearly universal and enduring source of social disruption and of the ruining, even taking, of lives. In our time, and I think for much of the coming century, the relationship of religion and ethnicity is going to form a principal source of disorder in the community of humanity. Many ethnic groups define themselves by appeal to God Almighty. And because right-thinking Americans, as well as people of good will elsewhere in the West, recognize the presumption and effrontery in that premise of social definition, such a definition is dubious.

Then what is the world of reason and goodwill to make of a religion that is universally described as ethnic, as Judaism is? And how are we to make sense of the claim of the faithful of that religion to believe in one, universal God, creator of heaven and earth, if at the same time those same believers form a tight little ethnic community, bounded by high and unsurmountable walls of genealogy and bonded by links of incomprehensible experience: the smell of their food, the rhythm of their dances. The world is too polite to ask, "So have you people made God your own tribe's god alone, and left the rest of us out?"

Too polite to ask, the world nonetheless has come to precisely that judgment of Judaism, and every account in secular language of the origins of Christianity, without exception known to me, contrasts the ethnic character of Judaism with the universal mission of Christianity. Not only so, but that secular description simply replicates and paraphrases the firm conviction of the earliest generations of Christians on the same point. As we will see in chapter 1, both ancient and contemporary witnesses to Christian truth say in so many words that what secured the triumph of Christianity and the ghettoization of Judaism was the ethnic basis of the latter, the universal appeal of the former. "No Jew or Greek" in Christ Jesus— that is what has (not unreasonably) led Christians to judge Judaism as ethnic and special and Christianity, by contrast, as the religion for the salvation of all of humanity. And since, everyone knows, Christianity took over the entire heritage of ancient Israel in the Old Testament, the conclusion is clear: Christianity supersedes Judaism because Christianity overcomes the enormous flaw in Judaism, its ethnicity.

The ethnicity of Judaism is supposed to derive from its emphasis on genealogy: birth into the people of Israel via a Jewish mother. A religion one gains by endowment at birth contrasts with a religion one enters by adoption through conversion or baptism; the one is ethnic, the other universal. The one makes distinctions by reason of birth, the other makes no distinctions among peoples or races or classes. That is the basis for the classification of Judaism as ethnic and of Christianity as universal. In this book I call into question the conviction that the paramount Judaism to emerge from antiquity, Rabbinic Judaism, conforms to the definition of an ethnic religion. I will show, to the contrary, that this religion defined the social entry formed by its faithful—Israel, the holy people—in terms at once theological and universal.

In fact, the narrow ethnicity of Judaism, contrasted with the welcoming universality of Jesus Christ's religion, forms a principal plank in the Christian polemic against Judaism constructed by the first generations of Christians. It is Judaism in the image of Christianity. But when a principal Judaism makes its own statement, as we will see, it invokes transcendental social categories to explain itself. That Judaism knows no barriers formed of race, language, and territorial location, and it is no more a circumscribed and ethnic religion than is Christianity. The same power to define humanity in God's image that Christianity in the first millennium of its history exercised from Finland to Spain and from England to Asia Minor found its counterpart in the power of Judaism to define a way of life and a worldview that governed quite comfortably from Spain to India and from Ethiopia to Norman York during much that same span of time.

To be Israel in that Judaism meant to live the Godly life in accord with the divinely revealed Torah of Sinai, and any human being who cared to come "under the wings of God's presence in the world" was welcome to join in that holy way of life. The Judaism that predominated from the early centuries of the common era (C.E., equivalent to A.D.) to our own day forms a religious system that is universal in focus and transnational in location and loyalty, receiving as equal all who undertake to accept "the yoke of Heaven" and "the yoke of the Torah," in the language of theology. A gentile enters that "holy Israel" of Judaism by a profession of faith, including baptism for women and men and circumcision in the covenant of Abraham for men. Once part of Israel, one is in no way meant to suffer discrimination or diminished status by reason of his or her origin elsewhere than in the communion of holy Israel.

To be sure, the children of Jewish mothers belonged by birth, not by a rite of entry, for the conception of Israel as an enduring social entity, deriving as it does from the scriptures of ancient Israel that Christianity calls the Old Testament, encompasses an ongoing social entity formed by appeal to common origin with Abraham and Sarah and their children through time. But that social entity is supernatural, formed by God's command and act, and whether its members have joined by birth or by choice, it is uniform and one. Any confusion between that transcendental Israel defined by the Torah and the this-worldly social entities formed of persons of common origin—any conception that Judaism is not a religion but merely a genealogy or that to be a Jew is innate and instinctual and racial—contradicts the explicit theology of the Torah.

So, it follows, two Judaisms meet in the pages of this book: the Judaism set forth by Saint Paul in Romans and the Judaism set forth by our sages of blessed memory (as these rabbis are called within the faith) in the Mishnah, Talmuds, and Midrash during the second through the fifth centuries of the common era. These religions did not coincide in time, since Paul's writing took place in the middle of the first century, while the oral part of the Torah was not written down until the formulation of the Mishnah, about 200 C.E., and the books of commentary to the Mishnah, called Talmuds, which were produced during the next four hundred years. So we do not deal with persons who met, but with arguments that persist. To the theological issues that preoccupy us, history proves monumentally irrelevant. People need not meet for their ideas to clash.

In these pages, I show that the Judaism of our sages of blessed memory—that dual Torah that they set forth out of the heritage of Sinai—knows only the transcendent, transcendental Israel that, for their Judaism, corresponds to the Jesus Christ, God Incarnate, of Christianity, born of that same heritage of Sinai. Here, where two religious systems intersect, a conversation can take place on this issue, each party appealing to evidence acknowledged as probative by the other.

Christianity enjoys the privilege of speaking first and of defining Judaism, including the Israel of Judaism, as it chooses. As a rabbi, I owe my guests the honor of framing the issue for discussion. Not only so, but Christianity, in the person of Paul, takes as a given the ethnicity of Judaism, contrasted with its own universality. So an account of Judaism in the model of Christianity, set forth by a Christian theologian, begins the book and defines the challenge to be met. The same challenge is accepted in the final chapter, being turned against the beliefs of the Jewish community nearest at hand to Paul. This Christian theological Judaism links the ethnic to the religious; Christianity itself breaks asunder the ethnic bonds that Judaism fastens around God. That is a standard and representative formulation of a standard Christian theological polemic. We will see that this polemic fabricates a Judaism that our sages of blessed memory will not have recognized as theirs. As I will point out, if Paul lived now in northeastern England and took a morning's trip from his home, he could assemble massive data in support of his characterization of Judaism. But, too, if he traveled not twenty minutes to the south, he would encounter a living community of Judaism that sustains my contrary characterization of the faith.

Accordingly, through the middle chapters of the book, I respond to Paul's characterization of Judaism. I do so not only as a scholar but also as a rabbi, aspiring to the honorable status of theologian on behalf of the Judaism that, as I have explained, has been and remains normative and vital. So—speaking after all in the twentieth, not in the first, century—I take as the Christian formulation of matters the most current authoritative statement I can find.[4] I set forth the Judaic presentation, however, in terms of how our sages of blessed memory, in the early years of the common era, conceived Israel, and whether, in their system, we can identify the basis for the distinction between the ethnic and the religious that defined the starting point of Paul's theology of Israel.

Paul wrote in the middle of the first century, while the documents of rabbinic Judaism derive from the second through the sixth; how then is it possible to formulate a debate between Christianity and Judaism? The answer, as I have already suggested, is that we compare systems to systems, placing them on a flat and shared plane beyond the specificities of temporal context. The comparison begins in the demonstration that the two distinct systems are comparable in categorical structure and the categories' functioning. The systems do permit comparison in terms of their own categorical structures for three reasons. First, both religions appeal to a common, authoritative source, and do so in much the same way; the hermeneutics compare. Second, both use the same categories—the definition of Israel being a prime example—to frame positions on the same issues. Third, both reach the same conclusions, though set forth in language particular to each religion and incomprehensible to the other. Conversation on matters formulated within a shared body of evidence, a common categorical structure, and a single heritage of faith in the revelation at Sinai certainly allows comparison and contrast of like to like (in search of the unlike), and that is precisely what I undertake in these pages.

Take Paul's perspective first. Critical to the Judaic system formed by Paul is the definition of Israel so framed as to make a place for gentiles who accept Christ, Israel's Messiah. Paul required an Israel out of the ancient scriptures that would accommodate newcomers in the new age that commenced at the resurrection. His Israel then had to accord full cognizance to the existing, known Israel "after the flesh," while distinguishing, within Israel, that Israel "after the promise" that gentiles now comprised, the promise having been kept in Christ Jesus. Finding in the Hebrew Scriptures a distinction between circumcision of the flesh and circumcision of the heart—at Deuteronomy 30:2, for example—Paul formulated a doctrine of Israel in two parts: ethnic Israel after the flesh, and spiritual Israel after the promise.

For a long time the rabbis represented by the Mishnah (ca. 200 C.E.) and the earlier Midrash compilations of the next century or so pursued their own issues in their own terms. Little that they said coincided with the concerns of the founders of Christianity. Each group pursued its own agenda, formed in response to urgent questions provoked by its own circumstances. Viewed with some perspective, the Judaic sages and Christian theologians formed two circles around a common point, the ancient scriptures, but in different spaces altogether, so not intersecting. Because they recognized Israel after the flesh as competition for the inheritance of the same holy scriptures, Christian thinkers gave thought to Judaism, but the Judaism with which they conducted their debates proved a fabrication. Drawn by their own fantasy, the Judaic sages, rather than inventing a Christianity with which to debate, preferred to conduct their discourse as if there was no Christianity at all and as if there was no other Judaism besides their own.

Formally, this same pretense—Christianity arguing with its own, chosen Judaism about its issues, Judaism going about its affairs as though Christianity never occurred—continued for the first millennium and then some. In the second millennium of the history of Christianity, a debate began, but each party continued to invent its own debating partner and demolish a position imputed to the other side.[5]

But we need not accept as final this formal formulation of matters. In fact, once we allow the contemporary re-presentation of Paul's theology of Israel to formulate the agenda for discussion, we find guidance to those important passages in the authoritative writings of rabbinic Judaism that respond to exactly the same issues, but, as I will demonstrate, in quite other terms altogether. Christianity and Judaism at certain points do speak to the same problem in a formulation that each party may comprehend in terms intelligible to the other. And since the definition and character of Israel, the people of God, takes priority in the respective religious systems, the possibility of an ethnic definition of Israel, which Christianity in Paul's formulation takes for granted and Judaism cannot conceive in any terms, defines a considerable debate.

Most of this book forms my address concerning normative Judaism's Israel, offered to Paul through an account of Judaism that recapitulates Paul's position on that same Israel. It reviews the three dimensions of the normative account of Israel: Israel as sui generis, beyond comparison with any other social entity; Israel as the children of Abraham, Isaac, and Jacob, Sarah, Rebecca, Leah, and Rachel; and Israel as elect, that is, as the people or nation to whom God was made manifest in the Torah—Israel as God's people, and Israel as God's stake in humanity and history. In each of these ways in which sages take the measure of Israel, I ask where and how an ethnic dimension may emerge, and I demonstrate that such an ethnic Israel lies beyond the comprehension of the Judaism of the dual Torah.

And this brings me to introduce myself and my interest in the matter. I am an American and a practicing Jew: an American whose religion is Judaism. My interest in Judaism is implicit in all that has been said to this point. I think Judaism (and Christianity) solved the dilemma of religion and ethnicity, and I maintain, also, that there is an American dimension to the solution of that same problem. I will spell out at the end what I think is to be learned from the Judaism of our sages of blessed memory and will point, also, to how I think our own country has learned something worth teaching to the rest of the world.

I offer both Judaism and Christianity as religions that have always meant to transcend ethnic boundaries, and I further invoke the remarkable experiment that is the American system. I regard the American system as the criterion for excellence, also, in religion: a way of allowing us all to listen to God's particular message in such a way as to turn toward, and not away from, the rest of humanity.

It remains to ask, is this an argument about long-ago issues and far-away disputes? I maintain the opposite. If we see Israel as ethnic and national-political, then we cannot make sense of much that happens within Israel. Let me offer a single example of how, outside of the framework of holy Israel—Israel seen as the Jewish people, a people called into being by God for the covenanted service that God has in mind for humanity—a deplorable event simply cannot be understood.

I take as my case in point the sin committed at Hebron in February of 1994, when a pious Judaist—a practitioner of Judaism—murdered Muslims at prayer. How are we to understand that event, and can we make sense of what happened in that framework of politics and sociology that ordinarily serves to explain who Jews are and what they do? In my view, to understand the massacre at Hebron, religion, not nationalism, best serves. Baruch Goldstein committed his act on the Jewish Festival of Purim. That was no coincidence. That Friday morning, with Jews throughout the world, he had read in the synagogue the Scroll of Esther. In accord with his (from his viewpoint) perfectly sane ideology, there he found instructions for his task that day: "So the Jews struck at their enemies with the sword, slaying and destroying; they wreaked their will upon their enemies" (Esther 9:5). The passage goes on to count up the number of those slain—five hundred here, seventy-five thousand there. "The next day was a day of merry-making and feasting." But on the day after Purim, the murderous ideology of Meir Kahane, which Goldstein mistook for the Torah of Sinai, produced only universal horror and shame for all faithful Jews.

Not Israeli nationalism, but a reading of the religion, Judaism, told Baruch Goldstein what he was supposed to do. From his perspective, within the community in which he lived, mass murder was a commendable deed. True, to the rest of us Jews, grieved at the sight of innocent people gunned down at prayer, it is an evil insanity.

But we err to call acts "insane" that in theological or ideological context are perfectly rational—within a given perspective. That explains why, when Collin MacPherson allegedly took out a gun and massacred white passengers on the Long Island Railroad, few dared blame the (to us insane) ideology of some blacks' hatred of whites. When Baruch Goldstein machine-gunned Muslim worshipers in

Hebron, few persons realized that the ideology of some Jews' hatred of gentiles explained the horror. The Muslim terrorists who blew up the World Trade Center carried out some Muslims' ideology of holy war against the Great Satan (aka the United States). David Koresh's conduct in Waco, Texas, made perfectly good sense to some Christians —those expecting Jesus Christ again and identifying Koresh with him.

MacPherson allegedly hated whites, and the to him reasonable ideology that whites are evil not only explained why he was miserable but also said what he had to do to exact just vengeance. So he took out a gun and shot up a train, making sure only whites would be his targets. The men who bombed the World Trade Center consulted not only books on how to make bombs, but also the Koran. Engaged in a holy war against the Great Satan, they learned their lessons at their local mosque and did what they were taught. Iranian foreign policy is built on the same conception of us. David Koresh presented himself as Jesus Christ come back and promised his followers not mass annihilation but the end of days. The expectation of the near-term end of history is common in important sectors of Christianity, even here in the United States. Had the federal agents understood Christianity as David Koresh represented that religion, the tragedy of Waco might never have taken place: they would have spoken his language and understood his motives.

The rest of us—blacks who reject racism, Muslims who believe in God as the All-Merciful, Jews who affirm the Torah's teaching that all humanity is made in God's image, and Christians whose Christ is the embodiment of love—dismiss as insane what to some of the faithful is virtuous. And that is because for many of us, faith profoundly held at the foundations of our very being yields not hatred but a kinship for the other, respect for the one who is different. The religious imperative, given urgency by the catastrophe of Hebron, is to search out the sources of the rational practice of mass murder, the reasonable and perfectly logical attitude of racial hatred, the sensible pursuit of the annihilation of those who are different. Where we are powerful, there we find our pathos. The power of racial self-respect to heal competes with the pathos of racial hatred directed against another; the power of religious service to God competes with the pathos of religious contempt for the outsider. Religion is God's gift to humanity—except when we turn it into Satan's curse. Religion without the humility that knowledge of the grandeur of God imparts, religion without the mercy that prayer for God's grace invokes—that is the religion that, in its narrowly ethnic and political forms, brings down a curse upon us all.

Acknowledgments

IN THE COOL FINNISH SUMMER, when the sun rarely set but seldom brought much warmth, I wrote this book amid the glowing hospitality of the Research Institute at Finland's Swedish-language university. It was, specifically, in my term as Gästforskarprofessor —Visiting Research Professor—at Stiftelsens för Åbo Akademi Forskningsinstitut and in association with my colleagues at Åbo Akademis Teologiska Fakultet. My dual position as research professor in the Research Institute and theological faculty member brought me into contact with a variety of Finnish professors and students, and I found not only a warm welcome but also much stimulating conversation in that intellectual community. My near-at-hand colleagues in the study of Judaism showed unusual hospitality, even by the high standards that prevail throughout Finland, and I express thanks to them all.

These words of thanks are for more than hospitality in general. My colleagues at Åbo Akademi discussed these chapters as I wrote them; they read each day's work as it emerged, commented on it, noted ways I might improve it, called my attention to books that would expand my knowledge and vision, and read later versions of the same chapters as they came forth. The partnership was detailed and concrete. Special thanks go to Professor Karl-Gustav Sandelin, who shared with me his learning on Philo, and to Professor Karl-Johan Illman, who read the manuscript and commented on it. I also thank Dr. Allan R. Brockway, then at Selly-Oaks Colleges in Birmingham, England, for his comments on the manuscript.

I express thanks to Stiftelsens för Åbo Akademi Forskningsinstitut for a very generous research stipend for April through August 1993 and for providing in addition comfortable living and working conditions. Among the research institutes at which I have worked, none exceeds the one at Finland's Swedish-language university in cordiality or hospitality.

Among many valued Finnish friends, both Finnish- and Swedish-speaking, I thank most especially my host and friend, Professor Karl-Johan Illman, for inviting me and making the visit memorable and happy. He made specific contributions to this book among the several I wrote or edited in his company, by calling to my attention important works that I might otherwise have missed. The many long walks his wife and he took with my wife and me around Åbo/Turku and the islands of its archipelago were enriched by their wise reflections about life in Finland and about our shared scholarly interests, and these walks found their way into the pages of this book and led to the many companions produced in my Finnish sojourn. Fortunate indeed are the Americans invited to pursue their scholarship in that sturdy and welcoming country; testimony to our appreciation of its virtues of hospitality and collegiality and learning is the number of Americans who return whenever they are able to live out life in the Nordic lands (especially in summer).

During this same span of time, I was invited to lecture at the fifth congress of the Scandinavian Congress for Jewish Studies, at Lund, and also for the theological faculty of the University of Lund. I express my thanks to my colleagues at Lund and also to those in Judaic studies throughout Scandinavia, who received me very cordially and responded to my lectures with penetrating and stimulating questions. During this same period I lectured for the Jewish communities of Stockholm, Uppsala, Helsinki, and Åbo, and I express appreciation for the warm hospitality my wife and I received there.

Because I used the opportunity to improve my Swedish, I express my appreciation, also, to the many patient Finns, both Finnish- and Swedish-speaking, who formed a language laboratory without walls for my continuing education in one or another of their languages. It was certainly one of the most interesting overseas summer terms I can remember, and one of the most pleasant and productive as well.

This book—moving back and forth across the frontier between historical scholarship and theological discourse—carries forward a series of exercises of mine intended to contribute to the future theological dialogue between Judaism and Christianity that I regard as essential for both religions. At stake in that dialogue as I think it should go forward are issues of faith, not merely secular social order. We are separated by what makes the other different: the oral part of the Torah, and the Torah's realization and fulfillment, Jesus Christ. But we are joined by the claim each makes that the Torah, or Christ, is from one and the same God, who is made manifest to us through one and the same act of revelation, recorded in the same Torah of Sinai and realized in that same covenant. And, as I will show, we also are joined by categories in descriptive and secular language that correspond and serve to gather data of a single sort.

I regard that dialogue as urgent and Godly—an act of service and loyalty to the God made known to the patriarchs and matriarchs of Israel and covenanted in love and in law through the community of Israel at Sinai. From Christianity, I learn potentialities in the Torah that I might otherwise not have appreciated; in return I want to contribute to Christianity the possibility of the knowledge of God through the Torah—the dual Torah set forth by our sages of blessed memory—which without Judaism, Christianity might never grasp. So I conceive the task of each to teach the other what it has learned about God through the Torah of Sinai (Christianity's Old Testament, Judaism's written Torah).

In this book I rely upon some of the findings spelled out in full in my *Judaism and Its Social Metaphors: Israel in the History of Jewish Thought*. While the issues are different, this book will go over sources that form an important part of the argument of the other. Each book stands on its own and addresses a problem distinct from that of the other, but the sources cited overlap.

My appreciation for the Judaism of our sages of blessed memory is deepened in dialogue with faithful Christians: Father Andrew Greeley, the great Roman Catholic sociologist; Bishop John Favalora, Catholic bishop of the Diocese of St. Petersburg, Florida;

and Reverend Dr. Bruce D. Chilton, Bard College, an Episcopalian priest, for only three examples. As this book goes to press, I prepare to serve as Bard Center Fellow at Bard College, so as to teach a course on the Judaeo-Christian dialogue with Professor Chilton. It is no surprise, then, that this book began in letters from Reverend Dr. William H. Scarle, Franklin Union Baptist Church, Worthington, Pennsylvania, whose comments on matters of Judaeo-Christian dialogue, in a spirit of love for the Torah and deep respect for Judaism, stimulated me to ask a variety of questions that I had never before contemplated. He made me reconsider the entire issue of ethnicity and Judaism (especially rabbinic Judaism), which this book addresses. He expressed to me in a moving way the importance he placed on being part of Israel, the Israel of the Torah of Sinai. It is a pleasure to acknowledge his stimulating thought and patient criticism of my ideas; I owe him thanks for provoking thought on matters I would not otherwise have understood as critical. For growth in the religious life, I find particular nourishment in dialogue with Bible-believing Christians, on the one side, and Roman Catholic cardinals and archbishops, on the other. Along with the rabbis who are important in my life—I mention Rabbi Joel Zaiman, Baltimore, and Rabbi Jonathan Sacks, London, in particular —I find authentic religiosity in these Christian friends and neighbors in God.

Finally, I express my thanks to the University of South Florida. This book takes its place in a continuous research inquiry. I wrote this book as part of my long-term labor of research scholarship, expressed through both publication and teaching at the University of South Florida, which has afforded me an ideal situation in which to lead a scholarly life. No work of mine can omit reference to the exceptionally favorable circumstances in which I conduct my research as Distinguished Research Professor in the Florida State University System at the University of South Florida. I express my thanks not only for the advantage of a distinguished research professorship in the Florida state university system, which for a scholar must be the best job in the world, but also for a substantial research expense fund, ample research time, and some stimulating and cordial colleagues. In the prior chapters of my career, I never knew a university that prized professors' scholarship and publication efforts and treated with respect those professors who actively and methodically pursue research. For me, that respect—at home in Florida and here in Finland—has been a new experience, and a productive one.

1

The Premise of
Paul's Ethnic Israel

IF I, A RABBI, could talk with Paul—meeting in a dimly lit, quiet
catacomb synagogue in mid-first-century Rome, just after Paul's
systematic theological essay called Romans had been completed but
before his martyrdom—I would ask him to talk about what, in his
system, most engaged me in mine. And that is Israel. And he would
agree to discuss that very subject, since here in Rome he had given
his life's deepest and best-composed thought to the meaning of
Israel and the place of gentiles in that Israel.

Out here, in the diaspora, whether in Athens for Paul or in the
paradise of St. Petersburg for me, far away from the land of Israel
with its great population of God's people, both of us would have
gained an acute consciousness that the world held a great, great
many gentiles. Because both of us have read where Scripture speaks
to God's creation of the entire world and all its people (not just the
land of Israel and its holy nation), the issue of who and what is Israel
is made vivid indeed by our circumstance in the capital of an empire
controlled by gentiles. And Paul's recent writing, composed in exile,
pondered the question that occupied me too: just what are we to
make of a world that God framed out of the Torah and yet in
contradiction to it?

For, we agree in the quiet of our secure and secret place, we both
are Jews and stand within the Israel of which Scripture speaks, and
we each propose to tell the world that we know precisely what that
Israel is. Not only so, but we are Jews within the same tradition; he
was educated to live in accord with the Torah as the Pharisees

1

taught it; I stand squarely within a reading of the Torah that derives from that same perspective on what it means to be a kingdom of priests and a holy people. So we care equally about the same things, in the same terms. Both of us revere as God's word precisely the same Scriptures: the Torah that God revealed to Moses at Sinai. Paul and I can argue, because we agree about so much.

And that is why he would consent to talk with me, a rabbi, about that matter of who and what is Israel, since, in his system, the issue of who is Israel took a place no less formidable than it did— and does—in mine. The catacomb then would have offered not only a safe, but also an appropriate, situation for conversation: a Jewish place for fellow Jews to meet, in defiance of a world we both concurred offended God.

Stepping from the first century into the twentieth, we may frame matters in more academic terms: is Judaism an ethnic religion? The whole of Christianity says yes. The authoritative statement of Judaism, I will show, says no. Most Jews today concur with Paul, though not for his reasons; their Israel is a genealogy, not a theology. Arrayed against my representation of matters, then, is Christianity and the bulk of contemporary Jewry. But the sides are equal, for I set forth what is written in the one whole Torah, oral and written.

That Judaism treated as ethnic what Christianity reshaped in universal terms defines the established fact in the study of both the Gospels and rabbinic Judaism. Most scholarship takes as its starting point the position that Israel in the Judaism of that time is ethnic, but the Gospel, universal. Christianity improved on Judaism by bringing to all the peoples of the world what had originally been kept for only one people alone. So for Judaism, or rabbinic Judaism, Israel refers to an ethnic group, a particular people, defined in this-worldly terms. The contrast between the ethnic Judaism and the universalist Christianity derives from the presentation of Israel by the apostle Paul.

But if two thousand years separate me and Paul, great scholarship fills the gap, and I turn to a believing Christian's exposition of the matters on which Paul and I should have conducted our debate. It is not for me to set forth an authoritative account of Paul's views; a great tradition of learning does the work properly. In defining Christianity, Christian scholarship invariably sets forth, also, its account of Judaism because the question that Christian theology finds premier and provocative is, Why the parting of the ways? Why did Christianity not take over Judaism and succeed within Israel, as it manifestly did not? And why did Israel not join with the gentiles before Christ's throne? Above all, why did the gentiles accept what Israel rejected? These questions form a considerable program of inquiry and thought for Christianity, and in one or another aspects of Paul's doctrine of Israel, the failure of Christianity in Israel and its success among the nations is to be accommodated.

The explanation of a failure that also marks success, a success that also underscores failure, is invariable: Judaism (that is, the remnant religion, after Christianity took its leave) was ethnic, Christianity, universal. The nations came to Christ through a Christianity that was universal. Israel remained aloof, because its Judaism was (merely) ethnic. Paul did not know in Rome what we now know, but the logic that guided him proved sound indeed: without the doctrine of an ethnic Israel, Christianity could not accomplish its purpose, which was and is the salvation of all humanity in the framework of the covenant of Sinai.

Judaism's Ethnicity and Dunn's Partings of the Ways

A single, current, and representative statement of this view of ethnic Judaism as against universalist Christianity, which defines the state of the question in today's learning, derives from James D. G. Dunn's *The Partings of the Ways Between Christianity and Judaism and Their Significance for the Character of Christianity.*[1] Dunn takes as his question the explanation of "how within the diversity of first-century Judaism, the major strand which was to become Christianity pulled apart on a sequence of key issues from the major strand which was to become rabbinic Judaism." The parting of the ways "began with Jesus, but without Easter and the broadening out of the gospel to the Gentiles," the break may not have taken place at all. I take Dunn's as a representative statement of paramount Christian views on the ethnicity of Israel the people and the ethnic character of Judaism as (merely) the religion of a given people.[2]

How, then, does Dunn explain the parting of the ways between Christianity and Judaism? He appeals to the particularity and ethnicity of Judaism, as against the meta-ethnic, universalizing power of Christianity to reach out beyond the ghetto walls of an ethnic Israel. Here is his language:

> For the Judaism which focused its identity most fully in the Torah, and which found itself unable to separate ethnic identity from religious identity, Paul and the Gentile mission involved an irreparable breach. . . .[3]
>
> Christianity began as a movement of renewal breaking through the boundaries first within and then round the Judaism of the first century. At its historic heart Christianity is a protest against any and every attempt to claim that God is our God and not yours, God of our way of life and not yours, God of our civilization and not yours . . . against any and every attempt to mark off some of God's people as more holy than others, as exclusive channels of divine grace.[4]

Dunn's premise is that Israel found definition in both an ethnic and a religious identity. Certainly for our own day his view must prevail, since a broad consensus maintains that Judaism is "the religion of the Jews," whatever that may be, and that the Jews form an ethnic group, with part of them (the religious part) also constituting a religious community.

But, as I will show, distinguishing the ethnic from the religious aspect of Israel for the Judaism of the dual Torah simply defies the evidence in hand. Our sages of blessed memory conceive no ethnic Israel distinct from a religious Israel and these are the sources that attest to the Judaism of which Dunn speaks. So what I find in Dunn's formulation of matters is the explicit claim that Judaism (or rabbinic Judaism) takes second place in the hierarchy of religions because it is ethnic, while Christianity overspreads the bounds of ethnic identification. That is profoundly anachronistic, and it is factually wrong and wrongheaded in its view of Judaism. But Dunn cannot be blamed for seeing what Jews today themselves perceive about their group. It is quite natural to see Judaism as an ethnic religion for in today's world Jews regard themselves as an ethnic group. If he makes the distinction between the ethnic and the religious Israel, well, so do we.

This distinction, however, is a retrojection of contemporary sociology and politics (for instance, American ethnic politics, European social policy in respect to ethnic minorities, and Israeli national ideology) into the theology of a Judaism of ancient times. The distinction in fact is theological, and it actually was made in antiquity —but not by rabbinic Judaism. It is a distinction critical to the apostle Paul, then taken over as a matter of simple fact concerning not Paul's system but the Judaism that contemporary scholarship assigns to the time of Paul and defines as his competition—then and now.

But what if *Israel* in the language of Judaism refers to an entity of precisely the same type as *church* or *mystical body of Christ* in the language of Christianity? Once the characterization of Judaism, or the Judaism under discussion, as ethnic falls away, what remains? I see two religions competing for one humanity in the name of one and the same revelation at Sinai. As much as Christianity presents an option to Judaists and to all humanity, so too does Judaism's mediation of the voice of God at Sinai echo across the whole world. The Gospel then becomes a way station en route to holy Israel at Sinai: a supernatural, not a sociological, realm of being, as Jesus suggests when he says, "I come not to destroy but to fulfill"— which can only mean, to carry out the Torah of Sinai.

Ethnic Jews and nearly all Christians simply do not grasp the meaning of Israel as a category. They see the social metaphor, Israel, as ethnic in the narrow, this-worldly sense of the word: a particular people, different from other people by reason of genealogy, customs, social traits, and the like. And so would be the case, were it not for a simple fact: ethnic identity is transmitted genealogically, or by territorial and cultural assimilation.

Let me make this point clear: there is a difference between a group defined as ethnic and one framed as religious, and the difference lies in the contrast between cultural and territorial assimilation into an ethnic group, on the one side, and religious conversion, on the other. I cannot become a Bulgarian or a Finn by a profession of faith or an act of allegiance alone. My past as an American remains always present, a barrier to the future I want for myself in Sofia or Helsinki. I cannot become a Finn or a Bulgarian in Rome, but I can become part of Israel (or the mystical body of Christ) anywhere in the world. My accent would mark me as an American if I spoke in Finnish or Bulgarian. To the Torah, I have no accent, whatever language I speak.

A place in Israel, so far as the Torah is concerned, is reserved for every gentile who accepts the unity of God and the yoke of the Torah, God's revealed will for humanity. Gentiles become Israel wherever they live, so long as how they live accords with the requirements of the Torah; they may speak any language, so long as their words are the professions of Sinai. With the rite of baptism (and circumcision for men), any gentile becomes part of Israel, with no past whatsoever, not even a genealogy, but only a future in Israel. Language, accent, cuisine, clothing, housing, occupation, way of life, worldview—these give way to a supernatural transformation, precisely as Paul understands conversion in the Spirit. So our sages maintain that all persons may find their way under the wings of God's presence; everyone is welcome to assume the yoke of the Torah and the commandments which stand for the kingdom of God or (in sages' language) of Heaven.

Let me make this point explicit. Our sages of blessed memory understand Israel to refer to all those who share the inheritance of Abraham and Sarah, who are called to the Torah, who dwell under the wings of the Shechinah—the Hebrew word for God's presence. Israel stands for the Judaism of the dual Torah—a supernatural entity, not an ethnic one. The distinction is critical when we consider the appropriate category for this Israel. Is Israel a this-worldly people, with customs and ceremonies and exotic ethnic foods, songs, and dances, or is it a supernatural social entity, a people called to form a holy community by God at Sinai, comparable to the church?

This Israel in Judaism forms the counterpart to the church or the nation of Islam, in Christianity and Islam, respectively, but not to the Albanians or the Italians or the Algerians or the Swedes. To become part of Israel, one affirms a faith; one need not undertake a long process of territorial, cultural, or ethnic assimilation. The entire corpus of the law of the Mishnah attests to the supernatural character of Israel—the very "Israel after the flesh" of which the New Testament speaks. This supernatural character is also suggested on every page of the prayer book of Judaism and in every pertinent line of the Midrash compilations and Talmuds. In the Judaism of the dual Torah Israel is no more a merely ethnic category than "Christ" is a merely political one (the king of the Jews) or the church is a merely sociological one (an institution). For rabbinic Judaism, Israel formed a category that was sui generis and supernatural; entering Israel by coming under the wings of the Shechinah bears nothing in common with joining an ethnic group.

Which Judaism: A Brief Account of the Sources

The particular Judaism set forth here requires its own definition to establish a clear frame of reference. Over the centuries, Judaic religious systems of various kinds have been expressed by particular groups of Jews and in their respective bodies of writing. We must therefore speak not of Judaism—there having been no single one through time—but of a Judaism, meaning a Judaic religious system. Only in that way shall we identify coherent data and avoid confusion.

As I have briefly mentioned in another context, by a religious system I mean a cogent composition of three things: (1) a worldview, (2) a way of life, and (3) a theory about the social entity making up the system. This ethos, ethics, and social theory raise fundamental and urgent questions and then answer those questions with cogent and (to the system's framers) self-evidently valid statements. Thus, a Judaic system will set forth an account of (1) a worldview, (2) a way of life, and (3) a social entity that defines the particular Israel for whom it speaks. The conceptions *Judaism* and *Israel* in the context of the diversity of Judaisms over time stand for what is negotiable, each Judaism telling its faithful who and what its Israel was meant to comprise. These conceptions will be easily grasped by Christians aware of the diversity of Christianities over time and in the world today.

Just as there is no Christianity without a clear account of Christ and the mystical body of Christ, or the church, so there is no Judaism without a definition of Israel, spilling over into who, and what, is a Jew. The identification of Israel has preoccupied thinkers of all Judaisms from the beginning to the present. The making of Judaic systems commenced with the formation of the Pentateuch in the aftermath of the destruction of the first Temple of Jerusalem in 586 B.C.E. From that time to the present day, the definition of Israel—who belongs, who does not, and to what sort of social entity do Israelites adhere in creating an Israel—has formed a remarkably pervasive theme in all Judaisms. When we take up the systemic treatment by a Judaism of the category *Israel,* we address a critical and indicative issue of the Judaic system under study. Given the diversity of Judaisms past and present, we cannot find it astonishing that the name for the social entity constituted by Jews, the name *Israel,* has carried a variety of meanings, and, as we will soon understand, each of these served not as a concrete description of real people living in the here and now, but as a metaphor. An Israel in a given system might enjoy no counterpart among social entities here on earth; this Israel would then frame its own metaphor. This social entity could constitute a family of a particular order—for example, all Jews descended from Abraham, Isaac, and Jacob, Sarah, Rebecca, Leah, and Rachel. Such a Judaism invokes the metaphor of family.

Or, it may be held, Israel constitutes a people or a nation, in which case to be Israel is to be part of a political unit of one kind or another, comparable to other such social groups based on, or in, a shared political being. This political metaphor will dictate thought on the nature of Israel, whether or not the Jews at a given time and place constitute a political entity at all.

We find, furthermore, the claim that the social entity at hand simply is not like any other, a genus unto itself. Israel as a unique entity has no counterpart among the nations—on one side of the social equation of humanity are all the nations; on the other side stands Israel, all alone. These and other metaphors serve as the vehicles for the social thought of the Judaic systems, or Judaisms, of the ages. How all this is to be reduced to an ethnic religion is not our concern here. What we have to find out is precisely how the normative Judaism—that Judaism set forth by the dual Torah—defined its Israel.

The Judaism of the dual Torah is what the world knows today as Judaism. It takes shape in the here and now of Orthodox Judaisms, both segregationist and integrationist, in the United States and overseas, as well as Reform, Conservative, Reconstructionist, traditional, and other Judaic systems that refer to the same documents as canonical. We will discuss these documents presently; first let us ask about the generative myth and symbol to which all formulations of the same normative Judaism appeal. As touched on earlier, I call this normative Judaism the Judaism of the dual Torah, because its principal symbolic statement invoked the myth that at Sinai God revealed the Torah, that is, the revelation, in two media: one in writing, today contained in the Hebrew Scriptures (for Christians, the Old Testament), and one formulated and transmitted orally, through memory.

That memorized Torah (commonly called oral Torah) is now written down, so this Judaism maintains, in the Mishnah, a philosophical law code brought together at about 200 C.E., to which the Talmud, meaning the Babylonian Talmud, forms the authoritative commentary. In fact, the memorized Torah in late antiquity encompassed a variety of writings. These writings form the sole evidence on the basis of which we may describe the Judaism of the dual Torah. They fall into two parts: first, those centered on the Mishnah; second, the ones that amplify Scripture. The former—dealing with the Mishnah—included the Tosefta, a corpus of supplements to statements in the Mishnah, organized around the framework of the Mishnah and expressed in the language and cadences of the Mishnah; the Talmud of the land of Israel, called the Yerushalmi, a systematic commentary to thirty-nine tractates of the sixty-two tractates of the Mishnah, brought to closure at around 400 C.E.; and the Bavli, or Talmud of Babylonia (ca. 600 C.E.), which comments on thirty-seven tractates of the Mishnah (and not the same ones addressed in the Yerushalmi).

The history of the Judaism of the dual Torah unfolded in two stages, marked off by diverse writings, now to be considered in sequence. Those writings fall into two groups, each with its own plan and program, the one produced in the second and third centuries of the common era, the second in the fourth and fifth. The first of these groups of writings begins with the Mishnah (ca. 200 C.E.) later on called the first statement of the oral Torah. In its wake, the Mishnah drew the tractate Abot (ca. 250 C.E.), a statement on the standing of the authorities of the Mishnah concluded a generation after the Mishnah; the Tosefta (ca. 300 C.E.), already mentioned;

and the three systematic exegeses of Scripture previously described: Sifra to Leviticus, Sifré to Numbers, and Sifré to Deuteronomy (concluded about 300 C.E.).

These books overall form one stage in the unfolding of the Judaism of the dual Torah. This stage stressed issues of the sanctification of the life of Israel, the people, in the aftermath of the destruction of the Temple of Jerusalem in 70 C.E. I call this system a Judaism without Christianity, because the issues found urgent in the documents representative of this phase address questions not pertinent to the Christian definition of Israel.

The second set of writings begins with the Talmud of the land of Israel, or Yerushalmi (ca. 400 C.E.), already described; Genesis Rabbah, assigned to about the next half century; Leviticus Rabbah (ca. 450 C.E.); Pesiqta deRab Kahana (ca. 450–500 C.E.); and, finally, the Talmud of Babylonia, or Bavli, assigned to the late sixth or early seventh century. The two Talmuds systematically interpret passages of the Mishnah, and the other documents, as mentioned, do the same for books of the written Torah. Some other treatments of biblical books important in synagogue liturgy, particularly the Five Scrolls (e.g., Lamentations Rabbati, Esther Rabbah, and the like), are supposed also to have reached closure at this time.

This second set of writings introduces the matter of Israel's sanctification, the matter of Israel's salvation, with doctrines of history and the Messiah given prominence in the larger systemic statement. This brief account of the documents that set forth the Israel and the particular Judaism under discussion here suffices to permit us to turn to the question of the ethnicity of this Israel.

Israel in the System of the Mishnah

The Mishnah's Judaic system gives Israel two identical meanings: the Israel of all the Jews here and now, but also the Israel of which Scripture—the Torah—spoke. These meanings encompassed both the individual and the group, without linguistic differentiation of any kind. Thus in the Mishnah Israel may refer to an individual Jew (always male) or to all Jews, that is, the collectivity of Jews. An individual woman is nearly always called *bat yisrael,* daughter of (an) Israel(ite). Sages in the Mishnah did not merely assemble facts and define the social entity as a matter of mere description of the given. Rather, they portrayed it as they wished to. They imputed to the social group, the Jews, the status of a systemic entity, Israel. To others within Jewry it was not at all self-evident that all Jews constituted one Israel, and that that one Israel formed the direct and immediate continuation, in the here and now, with the Israel of holy writ and revelation. As we will see, the Essene community at Qumran did not come to that conclusion, and the sense and meaning of Israel proposed by the authors of the Mishnah and related writings did not strike Philo as the main point at all. Paul, for his part, reflected on Israel within categories not at all symmetrical with those of the Mishnah. The Mishnaic identification of Jewry in the here and now with the Israel of Scripture therefore constituted an act of metaphor, comparison, contrast, identification, and analogy. It is that Judaism's most daring social metaphor. Moreover, the metaphor implicitly excluded a broad range of candidates from status as an Israelite—the Samaritans, for one example, and the scheduled castes of Mishnah-Tractate Qiddushin, chapter 4, for another. Calling (some) Jews *Israel* established the comprehensive and generative metaphor that gives the Mishnaic system its energy. From that metaphor all else derived momentum.

The Mishnah defines Israel in antonymic relationships of two sorts: first, Israel as against not-Israel, or gentile; and second, Israel as against priest, or Levite. Israel serves as a taxonomic indicator, part of a more encompassing system of hierarchization; Israel defined the frontiers on the outer side of society and the social boundaries within society. To understand the meaning of Israel as the Mishnah and its associated documents sort matters out, we consider the sense of the word gentile. The authorship of the Mishnah does not differentiate among gentiles, who represent an undifferentiated mass. To the system of the Mishnah, whether or not a gentile is a Roman or an Aramaean or a Syrian or a Briton does not matter. That is to say, differentiation among gentiles rarely, if ever, makes a difference in systemic decision making.

Likewise, Israel is not differentiated either. The upshot is that just as *gentile* is an abstract category, so is *Israel*. *Kohen* is a category, and so is *Israel*. For the purposes for which Israel/priest are defined, no further differentiation is undertaken. That is where matters end for the Mishnaic system. But to the Judaic system represented by the Yerushalmi and its associated writings, a gentile may be Roman or other than Roman, for instance, Babylonian, Median, or Greek. That act of further differentiation—we may call it *speciation*—makes a considerable difference in the appreciation of gentile. In the Mishnah authorship's Israel, therefore, we confront an abstraction in a system of philosophy. What we do not find is either the distinction between the ethnic and the religious or the conception that the Torah addresses only Jews of ethnic origin. The Mishnah's Israel is the same as Scripture's; its act of faith entails identifying the Israel of here and now with the Israel that stood at Sinai, and that is accomplished by recasting a one-time historical event into an all-time paradigm of Israel's existence, a transformation of time into an eternity in the present tense and in the world to come. The two meet in the reality of supernatural Israel. There is no Israel that is merely ethnic, only the Israel that is defined and comprised by each one who has a share in the world to come.

Israel in the System of Paul

Let us return to that quiet catacomb, where Paul and I sit together and talk of contentious matters. Can we talk at all? Yes and no: the categories are the same, but the contents scarcely correspond. What is unthinkable in the Mishnah is taken for granted by Paul. And that is hardly surprising. Just as the Mishnah's system makes no provision for the distinction between the ethnic and the religious, since such a distinction is, in the exact sense of the word, simply unthinkable, so the distinction between the promise and the flesh marks the point at which thought begins for Paul. It is systemically central.

The reason is simple. The generative problematic that tells Paul what he wishes to know about Israel derives from the larger concerns of the Christian system Paul proposes to work out. That problematic was framed in the need, in general, to explain the difference between those who believed and those who did not believe in Christ. But it focused, specifically, on the matter of Israel, and how those who believed in Christ but did not derive from Israel related to those who believed and also derived from Israel as well as those who did not believe but derived from Israel. Do the gentile believers have to keep the Torah? Are the nonbelieving Jews subject to justification? Had Paul been a gentile and not an Israelite, the issue would not have proved critical in the working out of an individual system (but only in the address to the world at large); we thus may take for granted that Paul's own Jewish origin made the question at hand important, if not critical. What transformed the matter from a chronic into an acute question—the matter of salvation through keeping the Torah—encompassed, also, the matter of who is Israel.

Paul appeals, for his definitive indicator of Israel, to a consideration we have not found commonplace at all, namely, circumcision. It is certainly implicit in the Torah, but recall that the Mishnah's laws accommodate as Israel any person who (for good and sufficient reasons) is not circumcised, and they treat as not-Israel any person who is circumcised but otherwise does not qualify. So for the Mishnah's system, circumcision forms a premise, not a presence, a datum, but not a decisive tacit indicator. One may be circumcised yet not enter the world to come. But Paul, by contrast, considered all those who are circumcised to be Israel, and all those who are not circumcised to be non-Israel—pure and simple.

That has been shown by Jonathan Z. Smith.[5] He states that "the strongest and most persistent use of circumcision as a taxic indicator is found in Paul and the deutero-Pauline literature. Paul's self-description is framed in terms of the two most fundamental halakic definitions of the Jewish male: circumcision and birth from a Jewish mother. . . .'Circumcised' is consistently used in the Pauline literature as a technical term for the Jew, 'uncircumcised,' for the gentile." It must follow, as I said, that for Paul, Israel is the circumcised nation, and an Israel is a circumcised male.[6] The reason for the meaning attached to Israel is spelled out by Smith:

> What is at issue . . . is the attempt to establish a new taxon: "where there cannot be Greek and Jew, circumcised and uncircumcised, barbarian and Scythian" (Col. 3:11), "for neither circumcision counts for anything but uncircumcision but a new creation" (Gal. 6:15).

For Paul, the matter of Israel and its definition forms part of a larger project of reclassifying Christians in terms not defined by the received categories, but as a third race, a new race, in a new story.

Smith proceeds to make the matter entirely explicit to Paul's larger system: "Paul's theological arguments with respect to circumcision have their own internal logic and situation: that in the case of Abraham, it was posterior to faith (Rom. 4:9–12); that spiritual things are superior to physical things (Col. 3:11–14); that the Christian is the 'true circumcision' as opposed to the Jew (Phil. 3:3) . . . But these appear secondary to the fundamental taxonomic premise, the Christian is a member of a new taxon."

In this same context Paul's letter to the Romans presents a consistent picture. In chapters 9 through 11 he presents his reflections on what and who is (an) Israel. Having specified that the family of Abraham will inherit the world not through the law but through the righteousness of faith (Rom. 4:13), Paul confronts Israel as family and redefines the matter in a way coherent with his larger program. The children of Abraham will be those who "believe in him that raised from the dead Jesus our Lord, who was put to death for our trespasses and raised for our justification" (Rom. 4:24–25). For us the critical issue is whether or not Paul sees these children of Abraham as Israel. The answer is in his address to "my kinsmen by race. They are Israelites, and to them belong the sonship, the glory, the covenants, the giving of the law, the worship, and the promises; to them belong the patriarchs, and of their race, according to the flesh, is the Christ. God who is over all be blessed for ever" (Rom. 9:3–4). Israel then is the holy people, the people of God.

But Paul proceeds to invoke a fresh metaphor, Israel as olive tree, to reframe the doctrine of Israel in a radical way: Not all who are descended from Israel belong to Israel, and not all are children of Abraham because they are his descendants . . . it is not the children of the flesh who are the children of God, but the children of the promise are reckoned as descendants (Rom. 9:6–7). Here we have an explicit definition of Israel, not after the flesh but after the promise. Israel then is no longer a family in the concrete sense in which, in earlier materials, we have seen the notion. Those Israelites of the flesh who pursued righteousness based on law did not succeed in fulfilling that law because they did not pursue it through faith (Rom. 9:31), "and gentiles who did not pursue righteousness have attained it, that is, righteousness through faith" (Rom. 9:30). There is an Israel after the flesh but *also* "a remnant chosen by grace . . .

the elect obtained it . . ." (Rom. 11:5–6), with the consequence that the fleshly Israel remains, but gentiles ("a wild olive shoot") have been grafted "to share the richness of the olive tree" (Rom. 11:17). Do these constitute Israel? Yes and no. They share in the promise. They are Israel in the earlier definition of the children of Abraham. There remains an Israel after the flesh, which has its place as well, and that place remains with God: "As regards election they are beloved for the sake of their forefathers. For the gifts and the call of God are irrevocable" (Rom. 11:28–29).

In other words, Israel expresses the main point of Paul's system. For Paul's Judaic system, encompassing believing gentiles but also retaining a systemic status for nonbelieving Jews, Israel forms an important component within a larger structure. More to the point, Israel finds definition on account of the logical requirements of that encompassing framework. Indeed, I cannot imagine making sense of the remarkably complex metaphor introduced by Paul—the metaphor of the olive tree—without understanding the problem of thought that confronted him, and that he solved through, among other details, his thinking on Israel. The notion of entering Israel through belief but not behavior (works) expresses the main point of Paul's system, which concerns not who is Israel but what faith in Christ means. The shape and meaning imputed to the social component, Israel, conform to the larger interests of the system constructed by Paul, both episodically, and, in Romans, quite systematically.

The Source of Judaisms' Definitions and Uses of Israel

Since, we recognize, late antiquity produced many Judaic systems and no single Judaism, we cannot generalize about the meaning of *Israel* in Judaism. Rather, we have to ask about the category *Israel* served in various Judaisms. For that purpose, we will take up the uses of *Israel* in the Judaic system outlined by the Alexandrian Judaic thinker Philo, and the place and importance accorded to *Israel* in the Essene library of Qumran. In this way we may gain perspective by comparing and contrasting how a number of Judaic systems made use of the same basic category. What we will learn is that these systems did not conform to a single pattern: in some,

Israel played a major role; in others, a minor one. That allows us to understand the importance accorded to *Israel* by Paul, on the one side, and the sages of rabbinic Judaism, on the other.

Is Israel important in every Judaism? The criterion for answering the question is simple. Were the entity or trait *Israel* to be removed from a given system, would that system radically change in character, or would it merely lose a detail? What is required is a mental experiment, but not a very difficult one.

First, without Israel, Paul simply would have had no system. The generative question of his system required him to focus attention on the definition of the social entity, Israel. Paul was a Jew but addressed both Jews and gentiles, seeking to form the lot into a single social entity "in Christ Jesus." His is the most ethnic Judaic system we have considered, simply because the issue of Israel focuses his attention and defines the solution to the problem he finds himself required to work out.

Second, without Israel, Philo, by contrast, would have done very well indeed. It was a detail of a theory of knowledge of God, not the generative problematic even of the treatment of the knowledge of God, let alone of the system as a whole (which we scarcely approached, and had no reason to approach!). We may therefore say that Israel formed an important category for Paul and not for Philo. Accordingly, the judgment of the matter rests on more than mere word counts, on the one side, or exercises of impression and taste, on the other. It forms part of a larger interpretation of the system as a whole and what constitutes the system's generative problematic.

Third, what about the Essene community at Qumran? When the library of the Essenes of Qumran takes up the issue of who and what is (an) Israel, it turns to what, to the authors, is its central question. Indeed, we may say that if the generative problematic of the Mishnah is defined by the exegesis of sanctification in the here and now of Israel's everyday reality, accounting for the excruciating detail to which the Mishnah subjects its audience, the precipitating issue of the Essene system revealed in the library of Qumran is defined by the exegesis in detail of us as Israel. And that issue holds together the principal documents and comes to expression even in a variety of fragments.

If, therefore, we ask whether Israel is critical to the Essenes of

Qumran, a simple fact answers our question. Were we to remove Israel in general and in detail from the topical program at hand, we should lose, if not the entirety of the library, then nearly the whole of some documents, and the larger part of many of them. The Essene library of Qumran constitutes a vast collection of writings about Israel, its definition and conduct, history and destiny. We cannot make an equivalent statement about the entire corpus of Philo's writings, even though Philo obviously concerned himself with the life and welfare of the Israel of which, in Alexandria as well as world over, he saw himself a part. The reason for the systemic importance of Israel among the Essenes of Qumran, furthermore, derives from the meanings imputed to that category. The library stands for a social group that conceives of itself as Israel, and that wishes, in these documents, to spell out what that Israel is and must do. The system as a whole forms an exercise in the definition of Israel as against that non-Israel composed not of gentiles but of erring Israelites. The saving remnant is all that is left: it is Israel.

The Source of Christianity's Distinction Between the Ethnic and the Religious in Judaism

I now turn to my conversation partner and say, "It is from you, Paul, that the Judaism that became Christianity has learned to distinguish the ethnic from the religious. And that is as it should be. But, I say to you without apology, the Torah as we have received it, through the chain of tradition formed by our sages of blessed memory upward to Sinai, makes no such distinction."

Paul replies, "Prove it. Prove it solely out of Scripture." Honoring Luther as I honor Paul, I agree, accepting the criterion of truth, *sola Scriptura,* but adding, "As our sages teach the Torah." And I will prove it—for Paul and for readers of the next three chapters.

But even now I underscore—in this conversation with Paul— that his is not the only reading of Scripture's Israel. The three Judaic systems briefly surveyed here—those of the sages of the Mishnah, Philo, and the Essenes of Qumran—know no such distinction and evince no capacity to understand it. The reason the distinction proved critical for Paul is self-evident. Paul found himself called to be a Jewish apostle to the gentiles; he did not propose to abandon his place within Israel (his Jewish identity, in anachronistic language to be sure). Whether or not the gentile church rests on the rejecting of Israel—one given up, the other substituted—is not at stake here.[7]

Nor do I mean to distinguish Paul from the rest of the Israel after the flesh or after the spirit in which he enjoyed kinship. I argue with Paul because I take him to be a formidable master of part of the Torah, the written part, just as generations of his heirs and continuators in Christianity have mastered the written part of the Torah in their way and for their purposes. I do not propose that Christianity stands beyond the shadow of Sinai, but that it means to take a long, long step toward the presence of God in the world. We argue about the meaning of the same Scriptures—Paul in his context, me in mine—because we appeal to Sinai together; we debate as a family about the shared heritage of the covenant set forth by the Torah of Sinai. We differ because we can agree about what matters.

Paul and the sages whose continuators produced the Mishnah both derived from the Pharisees, the former claiming that spiritual genealogy in so many words, the latter through a variety of no-less-explicit formulations. Both derived from the tradition of Gamaliel, thence from Hillel, his grandfather. Both understood that to enter the covenant God made with Israel, an act of conversion had to take place. Both wanted gentiles to come to the worship of the God who had revealed the Torah at Sinai. Both inherited the distinction between "circumcision in the flesh" and "circumcision in the heart" (Rom. 2:29), since Deut. 30:6 makes the distinction explicit. It follows that, in distinguishing the children of the flesh from the children of the promise, Paul certainly drew on an ancient and authoritative perspective of the Torah.[8] But it is also true that other Judaisms of the same time and place made no such distinction, nor, we will see, did the Judaism that became normative and reached full expression in the Talmud of Babylonia.

The upshot can be stated very briefly. While we may find in the three Judaic systems no distinction between the supernatural and the this-worldly—between holy Israel and ethnic Israel—we do find in Paul an effort to explore precisely that conception of differentiation. When we take for granted that we may distinguish the ethnic from the religious, we replicate the generative categories not of

Rabbinic Judaism but of Paul's system. The Judaism that focused its identity on the Torah recognized no distinct ethnic identity because it formed only a religious identity.

It was Paul who introduced in the analysis of Israel the distinctions within Israel between the ethnic and the religious that most scholarship takes at face value and then imputes to rabbinic Judaism. But as we have seen, mission to gentiles is an ongoing and important part of rabbinic Judaism (and of other Judaisms), and, once converted, a gentile becomes a wholly new creation, fully part of Israel. None of this has any bearing on ethnic considerations, and the distinction between the children of the flesh and the children of the promise points to no difference whatsoever that rabbinic Judaism ever contemplated.

All humanity is Adam, God's people one by one. But only Israel forms the counterpart to Adam, God's people all at once and all together. There are no peoples, there is only the people—the people of God, to whom all persons are called. As between Adam and Israel, the Torah is the issue. No wonder that Paul reflected so deeply on the relationship between the Torah and the definition of Israel. That he concluded that one distinguishes within Israel between the children of the flesh and the children of the promise hardly justifies historians, as distinct from theologians, in imposing the same distinctions.

This is, alas, the error of nearly the entirety of New Testament scholarship on the subject of Israel for Judaism and for Christianity—seeing as ever ethnic what Judaism sees as solely holy. If I could talk with Paul and persuade him to reconsider his Israel in light of mine, I might provoke him to reconsider issues critical to his larger system. But that conversation will have to go forward with Paul's heirs and continuators in various Christianities, all of whom concur on the ethnicity of Judaism. And why should they not, since vast numbers of Jews, in both the diaspora of the United States and also in the state of Israel, agree that Israel is not a sacred but a secular category.

They are wrong, all of them. For the Judaism of the dual Torah, Israel is a supernatural, not a this-worldly entity—as are God and the Torah. Now let us see how the Judaism of the dual Torah treats the same matter, Israel, in the three critical dimensions: sui generis, family, and people. Specific questions then follow, chapter by chapter: Chapter 2—What is Israel?; Chapter 3—Who is part of the family of Israel?; and Chapter 4—How does Israel the people (or nation) know and love God?

2

What Is Israel?

PAUL'S OPENING STATEMENT in our conversation is a simple one: there is no Jew nor Greek in Jesus Christ, but all are one. Ethnicity makes a distinction that, within Christ, makes no difference at all. Then we compare Jew to Greek: both appeal to an ethnic identity. The Jew possesses, in addition, a place in Israel, the people of God. That is by reason of the Torah. But the Greek may gain a place in that same people too. And that need not be through the Torah; it can be through Christ. Paul's Israel covers both the ethnic Israel, that is, Israel after the flesh, and also the spiritual Israel, that is, Israel after the promise. But when Jesus said he could raise up children for Abraham, he claimed no less than status as Israel. Then how do our sages of blessed memory respond? To find the answer to that question, we take leave of Paul's formulation and turn to the way in which various Judaic systems (Judaisms) deal with the question, Who and what is Israel?

Ethnic Identity and Religious Identity

Paul's comparison of individual Jews and Greeks contrasts with the formulation of Israel characteristic of the sages of Judaism. They know only Israel, the supernatural entity, the holy people; individuals simply exemplify and embody Israel. Their comparison is never Jew to Greek, always Israel to Rome.

If they never compare Jew to Greek, it is because their Israel falls into a different category from that formed by Greek, Median, Aramaean, Samaritan, Egyptian, and the like. First of all, Israel in their Hebrew speaks of the individual Israelite or Jew only in the setting of Israel the people or nation or family, so it would be difficult for them to formulate *Jew versus Greek* in terms of individuated person. The category is collective, even though it yields language to cover individuals. Any contrast involving an individual and his or her personal identity is beyond the conception of sages. They think in terms of large-scale entities. But are these entities ethnic? By *ethnic* I mean the group with which the individual identifies as a matter of genealogy and territorial identity or of language and culture.

By that definition, Israel does not form an ethnic entity at all. Nor is Israel made up of individual Israelites. Israel is a world empire; Israelites are its citizens, alike in their citizenship. Israel then contrasts with other empires, but not with other ethnic groups. While sages may treat their Israel as incomparable to any other social entity—a group that is unique in its groupness and that forms a classification unto itself—when they do speak of Israel in a setting of contrasts, the contrast will be drawn to either "the nations" without differentiation or to the four empires, Persia, Media, Greece, and Rome, with Israel as fifth and last in line. They may well contrast Israel with Rome and Iran, meaning the two world empires of their day. Their Israel, therefore, accommodates no definition that would assign a merely ethnic classification, such that would treat Israel in this-worldly terms at all. And, as we will see later, the same can be said for Israel as family. It is indeed a family, but like no other family on the face of the earth.

Because we invoked the most current characterization of Judaism as an ethnic religion, let us now systematically pursue the components of the sages' formulation of Israel and compare what we find in the sources with Dunn's account of the matter. Let us begin with the simplest question: precisely what sort of an entity do the sages conceive Israel to be? If they contemplate an ethnic entity, then how do they describe or define such an entity, in relationship to other such similarly ethnic entities in the world? How, then, do we deal with James D. G. Dunn's allegation that "for the Judaism which focussed its identity most fully in the Torah, and which found itself unable to separate ethnic identity from religious identity, Paul and the Gentile mission involved an irreparable breach"?[1] (See Chapter 1 for more on Dunn.)

In the preface of this book we began with a clear formulation, in precisely the terms of Israel's religious identity, and asked whether it accommodates an ethnic identity at all. We noted that Israel is elect by reason of its accepting the Torah and commandments—nothing ethnic here. These are precisely the terms of religiosity around which Paul's thinking about Israel revolves. But that proves only why Israel matters, not what defines Israel to begin with.

Then what about the ethnic dimension? As just discussed, the sages treat Israel as comparable to other entities, but these are not ethnic entities but meta-ethnic and multicultural: great political structures, empires. What we find here is the contrast between the great empires, Rome and Persia, and Israel. Individual Israelites (e.g., Abraham, Jacob, Joseph, and the like) stand for all Israel, and Israel stands against Persia and Rome, the world empires of the day. The issue is therefore not Greek versus Jew, individually. Paul can contrast Israel to gentile or to Greek because he is thinking about individuals. The sages of the dual Torah cannot, since they are thinking of world empires: Israel's counterparts are Rome and Iran. This they state in Genesis Rabbah.

Any conception that Christianity could not identify with a world empire crumbles upon the simple fact that, with the conversion of Constantine, Christianity entered into precisely the situation that Dunn assigns to Judaism when he says it was "unable to separate ethnic identity from religious identity." From that point onward, Christianity indeed found itself unable to separate imperial identity from religious identity, and in passages we will examine later, we will note that the same applies to the Judaism of that time. So while those who describe Judaism as ethnic are wrong about Judaism, they would in time turn out to be right about Christianity, which could not separate religious from imperial and political identity.[2] If Judaism was and is ethnic, then Christianity was and is political. But since most Christians understand that Erastianism destroys Christianity, they will also grasp why, to those of us who believe in the Torah, Israel is not and can never be ethnic. Note that I do not say "only ethnic." I deny at the very foundations the possibility that Israel can ever refer to a merely ethnic social entity.

What Is Israel? Comparable Entities: Adam in Eden, Israel in the Land of Israel

For Paul, Christ is the counterpart to Adam—the Adam to restore Eden, the one who did not sin and did not fall but who now restores humanity to its right relationship with God. For our sages of blessed memory, it is holy Israel that does precisely the same thing. So to understand Israel in Judaism, we have to grasp one critical definition of earliest Christology: Christ as the last Adam, a principal formulation for Paul.[3] Israel in Judaism is set forth as the counterpart to Adam, the land of Israel to Eden, the fall of Adam to the expulsion of Israel from the land. Whether or not Paul contemplated these paradigms when he formulated his Christology is not at issue; that the sages appealed to Scripture's models in framing their doctrine of Israel is self-evident.

The premise, that ethnic identity formed a component of the religious definition of Israel by rabbinic Judaism, falls away when we see precisely what rabbinic Judaism understood by Israel. That understanding emerges in a functional way when we ask ourselves what counterpart, in Christianity, we may identify to the rabbis' definition of Israel. The answer is, Israel for Rabbinic Judaism forms the counterpart and opposite of Adam. Humanity knows two stories, one of Adam in Eden, and the other of Israel in the land of Israel. These form counterparts. But they also mirror one another, for the Torah intervenes. Let us start with the comparison of Adam in Eden and Israel in the land of Israel, demonstrating that Israel's history in the land is comparable to Adam's history in Eden:

Genesis Rabbah XIX:IX

2. A. R. Abbahu in the name of R. Yosé bar Haninah: "It is written, 'But they are like a man [Adam], they have transgressed the covenant' (Hos. 6:7).

B. "'They are like a man,' specifically, like the first man. [We will now compare the story of the first man in Eden with the story of Israel in its land.]

C. "'In the case of the first man, I brought him into the garden of Eden, I commanded him, he violated my commandment, I judged him to be sent away and driven out, but I mourned for him, saying "How . . ."'[which begins the book of Lamentations and hence stands for a lament, but which, also is written with the consonants that yield "Where are you"].

D. " 'I brought him into the garden of Eden,' as it is written, 'And the Lord God took the man and put him into the garden of Eden' (Gen. 2:15).

E. " 'I commanded him,' as it is written, 'And the Lord God commanded . . . ' (Gen. 2:16).

F. " 'And he violated my commandment,' as it is written, 'Did you eat from the tree concerning which I commanded you' (Gen. 3:11).

G. " 'I judged him to be sent away,' as it is written, 'And the Lord God sent him from the garden of Eden' (Gen. 3:23).

H. " 'And I judged him to be driven out.' 'And he drove out the man' (Gen. 3:24).

I. " 'But I mourned for him, saying, "How . . .".' 'And he said to him, "Where are you" ' " (Gen. 3:9), and the word for 'where are you' is written, 'How.'

J. " 'So too in the case of his descendants [God continues to speak,] I brought them into the Land of Israel, I commanded them, they violated my commandment, I judged them to be sent out and driven away but I mourned for them, saying, "How . . .' "

K. " 'I brought them into the Land of Israel.' 'And I brought you into the land of Carmel' (Jer. 2:7).

L. " 'I commanded them.' 'And you, command the children of Israel' (Exod. 27:20). 'Command the children of Israel' (Lev. 24:2).

M. " 'They violated my commandment.' 'And all Israel have violated your Torah' (Dan. 9:11).

N. " 'I judged them to be sent out.' 'Send them away, out of my sight and let them go forth' (Jer. 15:1).

O. " ' . . . and driven away.' 'From my house I shall drive them' (Hos. 9:15).

P. " 'But I mourned for them, saying, "How . . ." ' 'How has the city sat solitary, that was full of people' (Lam. 1:1)."

There is an important difference between Adam and Israel, however. Israel and Adam are counterparts, but opposites; what Adam did not succeed in accomplishing, Israel realized in abundance: obedience to the Torah. Adam and Israel are comparable but not wholly alike. They are the same and not the same. The reason is that Israel has the Torah, which presents Israel with the possibility of escaping from the situation of guilt and alienation from God in which Adam is trapped. True, Israel's history in the land is the counterpart of Adam's history in Eden; with the destruction of Jerusalem in 586, Israel was driven out of Eden. But Israel can come back.

The difference between the situation of Adam and the situation of Israel finds its definition in the Torah. Christ on the cross concludes the old Adam and in his resurrection commences the new. Here we find the Judaic counterpart to that enormous conception. It is the Torah that forms the antidote to Adam's sin. Israel has to regain the land, that is, Eden, by the act of reconciliation with God that takes place through voluntary obedience to the covenant, the Torah, the commandments. Then Israel overcomes the situation of Adam; the Torah provides the occasion, but only Israel, the actuality. At this point, in this context, we have to ask ourselves how any aspect of this language speaks of an ethnic identity. Forming the counterpart to Adam defines Israel in much the same way that the last Adam is defined as counterpart and opposite to the first one, and the Last Adam is no more a this-worldly and secular figure than Israel is ethnic. How the category, *ethnic,* fits into the present context is not at all clear. *Israel is God's people* is no more ethnic a statement than *Adam stands for humanity.* Israel and Adam form species of the same genus, and what speciates them is the Torah.

Israel as a Taxonomic Indicator in the Mishnah

It does not suffice to identify Israel as merely other than an ethnic entity. We have to define the term as various documents use it, so that we may see with great clarity how Judaism's canon understood *Israel.* Only in this way will we realize how the categorization of Judaism as an ethnic religion simply misrepresents the theological facts of that religion. *Israel* stood for many things—as, in Christianity, did Christ. But the one thing that the word never suggests, in the rabbinic literature, is an ethnic, as distinct from a religious, entity or identity. So to formulate a counterpart to Paul's theory of Israel, we have to inform ourselves on how various Judaic documents understood the same category.

Take, for example, the utterly intangible and asocial framework in which Israel figures in the Mishnah. The Mishnah formulated its data in classifications seeking the rules that order all things. These emerge, as they do for Aristotle's natural history, by appeal to points in common or in contrast. Like things follow the same rule; unlike, the opposite. Order consists in knowing the classification of things; truth, in recognizing the hierarchy of all being, reaching upward to the One, flowing downward from the One to the many.

We should not, therefore, find surprising the fact that in the Mishnah, *Israel* serves as a taxonomic indicator, just as *woman* does. Israel's traits dictate relationships or derive from relationships. Israel exists therefore in relationship, not on its own as an entity bearing its own weight and establishing its own presence. Israel is important in dictating the outcome of relationships, not when it is subjected, in its own absolute terms, to description and analysis. The character of the definition of Israel in the Mishnah and associated writings indicates the importance accorded to the category.

That definition, as we will now see, proves negative, transitive, and merely relational, rarely positive and almost never substantive. The word and category *Israel* reach definition in relationship to other species of its genus: if nation, then Israel/not gentile; if caste, then Israel/not priest. These definitions viewed in this-worldly terms self-evidently tell us much about what Israel *is* when compared with other nations or other castes, but nothing about what Israel *is*. That is what I mean by *Israel* as transitive and not intransitive. To the use of *Israel* in the Mishnah, Paul's formulation is—not surprisingly—simply irrelevant, entirely out of phase and beyond all comprehension. *Israel after the promise* or *Israel after the flesh* set forth formulations without any meaning at all; in this context, they are pure gibberish.

In the Mishnah the premise of all discourse is that the entirety of the Jews' society is Israel. In the system of the Mishnah, the word *Israel* bears no autonomous meaning. Quite to the contrary, *Israel* for the Mishnah and related writings ordinarily finds definition in its opposite, whatever the antonym is. It is in the deepest sense a transitive category. Not only so, but the classifications important later on, which do bear autonomous and intransitive meaning, play little or no role in the earlier phase in the unfolding writings. *Is-*

rael/not gentile and *Israel/not priest* prove remarkably common senses of the word. Strikingly, Israel as family and Israel as sui generis, critical to the second phase in the matter, make at best cameo appearances. *Israel* therefore serves, as I suggested earlier, as a systemic classifier. That of course conforms to the larger purpose of the Mishnah's authorship, with its powerful concern for giving things their rightful name and placing them in their correct category and subjecting them all, each to its own intrinsic rule.[4]

Not only so, but the antonyms shift from context to context. So the word is not only defined in relationship to other words and not as an autonomous category, but it also takes on a variety of meanings, each relative to its context. An *Israel* does not serve, therefore, as a categorically definitive matter in the way that *Sabbath, writ of divorce, goring ox, priestly ration,* and *pot* constitute definitive categories, each with a fixed and permanent meaning. That is to say, while the meaning of *Sabbath* or *goring ox* does not change from setting to setting, the sense imputed to *Israel* undergoes remarkable shifts and changes. Consequently, the word finds meaning solely in relation to other words, in ways in which the names of the structural categories of the Mishnah's system do not. Nothing in Paul's usage of the word corresponds, since in every passage, he has a well-defined, intransitive entity in mind: an ethnic group, not an empire, and not a taxon, either.

If Paul had written a mishnah, it would have included ample definition of who is and who is not Israel. But the Mishnah as a whole has no division or even tractate devoted to the word *Israel,* meaning, in its context, who is an Israelite and who is not, what may one do or not do because he or she is an Israelite, and how (an) Israel functions in any of the settings so lovingly described in rich detail by the jurisprudential philosophers of the Mishnah. Information on all of these questions will prove abundant—but episodic and epiphenomenal. In short, an Israel may be one of two things. *Israel* may refer to a social entity, a social group defined by shared norms and traits imputed and expressed, in contradistinction to all other social entities of the same genus; that is, a unique species of a common genus, people or nation, Israel as against not-Israel. Or *Israel* may refer to a caste, a kind of class defined by genealogy and endowed with economic and social traits of differentiation, in contradistinction to all other castes of the same genus; that is, a unique species of a common genus, one level within the hierarchy of the social group, Israel as against priest, Levite, proselyte, and the like, but, most commonly, Israel[ite in caste], not priest[ly caste]. The classification, of course, pertains to the individual or to the group, without distinction. *Israel* within the people stands for a caste, and *Israel* among the nations stands for a nation; these meanings yield essentially the same thing, the one within the borders of society, the other outside. In both cases *Israel* constitutes a mode of hierarchization within a system that, at its foundations, constitutes a massive exercise in hierarchization.

That is why when *Israel* stands alone, not as a qualifier or partitive, in the Mishnah and successor writings it ordinarily functions as a contrastive; that is, Israel *and not an outsider,* or Israel *and not a higher caste.* Those are the two meanings associated with *Israel* in the principal document that came to closure prior to the end of the third century. If the author of the Mishnah heard *Israel,* they might think of the opposite as *gentile* (or *Samaritan* or *heretic*), or as *priest* or *Levite.* All senses of the word *Israel* in the Mishnah fall within one or the other classification.

Israel as Sui Generis in the Mishnah

For Paul, Israel is an ethnic entity, like any other ethnic entity. For our sages of blessed memory, Israel stands for a unique entity, unlike any other, not comparable to any other. Israel is not a category that possesses a counterpart; Israel is unique because Israel forms its own genus—that is, it is sui generis. That position is diametrically opposed to Paul's.

When we ask the authorship of the Mishnah to tell us in explicit terms how they define (an) Israel, they direct our attention to the one passage in which they systematically answer that question. It is framed, as a question of social definition must be, in terms of who is in and who is out. (An) Israel then is defined within the categories of inclusion and exclusion, which implicitly yields the definition that all who are out are out and all who are in are in, and that the ones who are in constitute the social entity or social group at hand. When the Mishnah's authorship wishes to define Israel by itself and on its own terms, rather than as a classification among other classifications in an enormous system of taxonomy, Israel may be set forth as an entity not only in its own terms but also sui generis. The context, however, will be defined by supernatural considerations.

The matter before us forms a powerful refutation of the proposition that, in this Judaism, Israel ever is a merely secular ethnic entity or may be broken down into religious and secular ethnic components in the way that Paul wishes to do. For when we take up the case in which Israel is sui generis, we find that its unique traits are wholly theological. What characterizes an entity that is sui generis will be traits pertinent only to that entity; for the case at hand, the categories are defined in terms of belief: affirming a given doctrine, denying another. That fact bears in its wake the implication that Israel as a social entity, encompassing each of its members, is defined by reference to matters of correct doctrine. All Israelites—persons who hold the correct opinion—then constitute Israel.

I know of no passage of the Mishnah and its related literature that is more concrete and explicit than the following passage on who is in and who is out. But the in group is not within this world at all. It is made up of those who enter or have a share of the world to come. Thus all those Israelites who constitute in themselves the social entity, the group Israel, form a supernatural, not merely a social, entity—and no wonder all metaphors fail. Gentiles who enter Israel gain the world to come, not a place in a merely this-worldly ethnic entity.

The premise is that we speak only of Israel, and the result is the definition of Israel in terms we should not have anticipated at all: not Israel as against non-Israel (the gentile) nor Israel as against non-Israel (the priest), but Israel as against those who deny convictions now deemed explicitly, indicatively, and normatively to form the characteristics of Israel. Here is an Israel that, at first glance, is defined not in relationships but intransitively and intrinsically—contrary to my allegations just a few pages ago. But that impression will soon shift, for Israel now invokes non-Israel, just as it did earlier, but for a different purpose and in a separate context. What this means, therefore, is that Israel is not a social entity at all like other social entities, but an entity that finds definition, as to genus and not species, elsewhere. To state the result simply: in what follows, Israel is implicitly sui generis. The passage, which was quoted in a different context in Chapter 1, is sufficiently important to warrant a recapitulation:

Mishnah-Tractate Sanhedrin 10:1

A. All Israelites have a share in the world to come,

B. as it is said, "Your people also shall be all righteous, they shall inherit the land forever; the branch of my planting, the work of my hands, that I may be glorified (Isa. 60:21)."

C. And these are the ones who have no portion in the world to come:

D. He who says, the resurrection of the dead is a teaching which does not derive from the Torah, and the Torah does not come from Heaven; and an Epicurean.

E. R. Aqiba says, "Also: He who reads in heretical books,

F. "and he who whispers over a wound and says, 'I will put none of the diseases upon you which I have put on the Egyptians, for I am the Lord who heals you' (Exod. 15:26)."

G. Abba Saul says, "Also: He who pronounces the divine Name as it is spelled out."

As we noted in Chapter 1, Israel here is defined inclusively: to be Israel is to have a share in the world to come. No other social entity in the Mishnah is defined this way, and so, for the authors of the Mishnah, Israel is sui generis. The Mishnah does not define Israel inclusively only, however. Those who reject the stated beliefs of Israel exclude themselves:

Mishnah-Tractate Sanhedrin 10:2

A. Three kings and four ordinary folk have no portion in the world to come.

B. Three kings: Jeroboam, Ahab, and Manasseh.

C. R. Judah says, "Manasseh has a portion in the world to come,

D. "since it is said, 'And he prayed to him and he was entreated of him and heard his supplication and brought him again to Jerusalem into his kingdom' (2 Chron. 33:13)."

E. They said to him, "To his kingdom he brought him back, but to the life of the world to come he did not bring him back."

F. Four ordinary folk: Balaam, Doeg, Ahitophel, and Gehazi.

Not only persons, but also classes of Israelites are specified, in all cases contributing to the definition of (an) Israel. The excluded classes of Israelites bear in common a supernatural fault, which is that they have sinned against God.

We begin with those excluded from the world to come who are not Israel, namely, the generation of the flood and the generation of the dispersion. This somewhat complicates matters, since we should have thought that at issue in enjoying the world to come would be only (an) Israel. It should follow that gentiles of whatever sort hardly require specification; they all are alike. But the focus of what follows—classes of excluded Israelites, who have sinned against God—leads to the supposition that the specified gentiles are included because of their place in the biblical narrative. The implication is not that all other gentiles enjoy the world to come except for these, and the focus of definition remains on Israel, pure and simple. If Israel is to be divided, it is not between ethnic and religious components, but among religious components.

Israel as Sui Generis in Leviticus Rabbah and in the Talmud of the Land of Israel

In Leviticus Rabbah the conception of Israel as sui generis reaches expression in an implicit statement that Israel is subject to its own laws, which are distinct from the laws governing all other social entities. These laws may be discerned in the factual, scriptural record of Israel's past, and that past, by definition, belonged to Israel alone. It followed, therefore, that by discerning the regularities in Israel's history, implicitly understood as unique to Israel, sages recorded the view that Israel, like God, was not subject to analogy or comparison. Accordingly, while not labeled a genus unto itself, Israel is treated in that way.

If I had to point to the single most common way in which sages made the implicit statement that Israel is sui generis, I would point to their "as-if" mode of seeing Israel's reality. Sages read Israel's history not as it seems—that is, not as it would appear when treated in accord with the same norms as the histories of other social entities—but as a series of mysteries. The facts are not what appearances suggest. The deeper truth is not revealed in those events that happen to Israel and to (other) nations over the face of the earth. What is really happening to Israel is wholly other, different from what seems to be happening and what is happening to ordinary groups. The fundamental proposition pertinent to Israel in Leviticus Rabbah is that things are not what they seem. Israel's reality does not correspond to the perceived facts of this world.

The exegetes maintained that a given statement of Scripture, in the case of Leviticus, stood for and signified something other than that to which the verse openly referred. It was a given for these exegetes that, for example, water stands for Torah, and the skin disease mentioned in Leviticus 13, in Hebrew called *saraat* and often mistranslated as "leprosy," stands for evil speech. What is decisive for our inquiry is that this mode of thought pertained to Israel alone. Solely in the case of Israel did one thing symbolize another, speak not of itself but of some other thing entirely. When other social entities (e.g., Babylonia, Persia, or Rome) stood for something else, it was in relationship to Israel and in the context of the metaphorization of Israel. When treated in a neutral context, by contrast, we find no metaphors. When Greece appears in the sequence of empires leading finally to the rule of Israel, then Greece may be symbolized by the hare. And there is another side of the matter too. Other things—the bear, the eagle—could stand for the empires, but—in that metaphorical context—then Israel stands only for itself.

Whichever way we have it, therefore, implicit in that view and mode of thought is the notion of Israel as sui generis, lacking all counterpart or parallel entity for purposes of comparison and contrast. The importance of the mode of reading Scripture as if it meant something else than what it said, in the case of the exegesis of Leviticus Rabbah, should not be missed. What lies beneath or beyond the surface—there is the true reality, the world of truth and meaning. Because the exegetes applied this mode of thought solely to Israel and not to the nations, it follows that Israel constituted an entity that was sui generis.

The doctrinal substance of the theory of Israel as sui generis may be stated in a single paragraph. Here is what our sages maintain: God loves Israel, so gave them the Torah, which defines their life and governs their welfare. Israel is alone in its category (sui generis), proved by the fact that what is a virtue to Israel is a vice to the nation; what is life-giving to Israel is poison to the gentiles. True, Israel sins, but God forgives that sin, having punished the nation on account of it. Such a process has yet to come to an end, but it will culminate in Israel's complete regeneration.

Meanwhile, Israel's assurance of God's love lies in the many expressions of special concern for even the humblest and most ordinary aspects of the national life: the food the nation eats, the sexual practices by which it procreates. These life-sustaining, life-transmitting activities draw God's special interest, as a mark of his general love for Israel. Israel then is supposed to achieve its life in conformity with the marks of God's love. These indications also signify the character of Israel's difficulty at the time the laws were written—namely, subordination to the nations in general and to the fourth kingdom, Rome, in particular. Both food laws and skin diseases stand for the nations. There is yet another category of sin, also collective and resulting in collective punishment, and that is social sin.

The moral character of Israel's life, the treatment of people by one another, the practice of gossip and small-scale thuggery—these too draw down divine penalty. The nation's fate therefore corresponds to its moral condition. The moral condition, however, emerges not only from the current generation. Israel's richest hope lies in the merit of its ancestors, thus in the scriptural record of the merits attained by the founders of the nation, those who originally brought it into being and gave it life. To none of these statements does the category *ethnic* pertain; all of them concern a theological definition of Israel, pure and simple.

Accordingly, the mode of thought brought to bear on the theme of Israel, now with reference to Israel's unique history, remains exactly the same as in the Mishnaic stratum: classification, accomplished through list making, with data exhibiting similar taxonomic traits drawn together into lists based on common monothetic traits or definitions. But the outcome of the inquiry into the social rules of Israel viewed as a problem in natural philosophy is not the same as in the Mishnaic system. Where the making of rules yielded an Israel in genus like, and in species unlike, other social entities, the discovery of rules produced an Israel that was sui generis. The lists, through the power of repetition, make a single enormous point and prove a social law of history.

This brings us back to Scripture, shared among our sages, Jesus, and Paul. The catalogs of exemplary heroes and historical events provide sages with a model of how contemporary events are to be absorbed into the biblical paradigm unique to Israel. Since biblical events exemplify recurrent happenings—sin and redemption, forgiveness and atonement—they lose their one-time character. At the same time and in the same way, current events find a place within the ancient, but eternally present, paradigmatic scheme. So no new historical events, other than exemplary episodes in the lives of heroes, demand narration because, through what is said about the past, what was happening while the framers of Leviticus Rabbah were at work would also come under consideration.

This mode of dealing with biblical history and contemporary events produces two reciprocal effects. The first is the mythicization of biblical stories—their removal from the framework of ongoing, unique patterns of history and sequences of events and their transformation into accounts of things that happen all the time. The second is that contemporary events lose all of their specificity and enter the paradigmatic framework of established mythic existence. So the Scripture's myth happens every day, and every day produces a reenactment of the Scripture's myth. The same cannot be said of a unique entity. If we speak of an entity unlike all others, then, by rights, we should not be able to make intelligible statements. But, as we see, sages can and do.

In their reflection on Israel as a unique entity, the authorship of Leviticus Rabbah pursued knowledge much as did philosophers, indeed, natural philosophers. Greek science focused on physics; the laws of Israel's salvation serve as the physics of the sages. But Greek science derived facts and built theorems on the basis of other sources besides physics. The Greek philosophers also, after all, studied ethnography, ethics, politics, and history. As a matter of fact, what made Greek science a true science was its power of generalization, of following curiosity beyond the case at hand. For the sages, parables, exemplary tales, and completed paragraphs of thought deriving from other sources (not to exclude the Mishnah, Tosefta, Sifra, Genesis Rabbah, and other such literary compositions that had been made ready for the Talmud of the land of Israel)—these too make their contribution of data subject to analysis. All of these sources of truth were directed toward the discovery of the philosophical laws of history. But these laws were for the understanding of Israel's life, now and in the age to come, and they concerned all of humanity only through the anthropology beginning with Israel as the counterpart and opposite of the fallen Adam. In so stating, we have moved far beyond our original inquiry because we have discovered, not for the first time, how theological sociology leads us backward toward that theological anthropology that—in the Judaism of the dual Torah—weighed in the balance the first Adam against Israel and found in Israel (not the social entity but the model and likeness) "in our image, after our likeness," what it meant to be human, like God. These observations carry us far beyond the limits of this book to an inquiry into the personality of God and the theological metaphors of Judaism.

As we find the rules of nature by identifying and classifying facts of natural life, so we find the rules of Israel's society by identifying and classifying the facts of Israel's social life. In both modes of inquiry we make sense of things by bringing together like specimens and finding out whether they form a species, then bringing together like species and finding out whether they form a genus—in all, classifying data and identifying the rules that make the classification possible. That sort of thinking lies at the deepest level of list making, which is, as I said, the work of offering a proposition and facts (for social rules) as much as a genus and its species (for rules of nature). Once discovered, the social rules of Israel's national life yield explicit statements, such as that God hates the arrogant and loves the humble. The readily assembled syllogism is as follows: If one is arrogant, God will hate him or her, and if one is humble, God will love him or her.

The case I proposed at the outset is this: Israel is conceived to be sui generis, and a systemic teleology amply expresses that conception. Israel would be saved through the Torah, and through individuals, by adherence to the Torah. This affords gentiles an entirely integral place in Israel. Within Israel, there is no Greek nor Jew, but only the holy people, all together. And this leads us to the final point, the place of gentiles.

What About Gentiles? What About Christians?

The Mishnah does not differentiate among gentiles, regarding them all as an undifferentiated mass in contrast to its Israel. When a gentile becomes part of Israel, it makes no difference whence he or she originated. There is only Israel, and Israel overcomes all prior difference. Israel then functions for our sages the way Christ does for Paul, and in Christ there is neither Jew nor gentile, free nor slave, female nor male, but all are one. Hence, for the framers of the Mishnah and its successor documents, the conception of Israel as an ethnic group distinguished from other such groups of the same classification is simply unthinkable. Dunn's category falls entirely outside the framework of reality for the Judaism portrayed here.

Let me make this matter concrete by asking a specific question. Does the authorship of the Mishnah differentiate when speaking of gentiles? The answer is no, for the gentiles represent an undifferentiated mass. To the system of the Mishnah, whether or not a gentile is a Roman or an Aramaean or a Syrian or a Briton does not matter (except, for example, at M. Neg. 2:2, as to skin tone—an Ethiopian is different from a German). Israel is not differentiated either. The upshot is that just as *gentile* is an abstract category, so is *Israel*. *Kohen* is a category, and so is *Israel*. For the purposes for which Israel/priest are defined, no further differentiation is undertaken. That is where matters end.

In this same context it suffices to take note of the slight importance accorded in the program of the Mishnah and successor documents to issues critical to Christianity. At no point can I discern in the Mishnah an interest in issues that differentiated the one Israel from the other, the old, after the flesh (so the new said) from the new, after the spirit. We look in vain for appeal in the Mishnah, even in the Sifra and the two Sifrés, to the meaning of being Israel after the flesh, that is, Israel as the extended family of Abraham and Sarah. The sages' Israel would not form a counterpart and opposite to that of Christianity before the advent of the Christian empire, Rome. Then, as we will see, we may construct a doctrine of Israel that meets head-on the formulation of Paul (among many) in Christianity.

In contrast, Israel as a category defined without attention to, or interest in, issues vital to the Christian opposition in the second and third centuries took on a form of its own. That form, imparted by the chosen via negativa of not-gentile, not-priest, discovered its repertoire of possibilities from the generative question of sanctification: who is holy Israel? Not the gentile. What is the holiest caste, in contrast to Israel as not-Israel? The priest. These issues come to the fore when we take as our critical question the issue of sanctification, its outer limits, its interior degrees and gradations. That is why Israel in the Mishnah forms an issue defined in terms to which Christianity simply proves irrelevant.

That was because, into the sages' view of things, Christianity scarcely entered. Paul can have taken on a sage of the dual Torah, since from the perspective of his system, the encounter compelled attention. But sages at this point in their writings produce nothing that suggests an argument concerning Israel with Christianity came under consideration. I cannot say whether or not the reason was that Christians were not numerous or not threatening or for other reasons not to be taken seriously. All our evidence tells us only that, in the view of the authorship of the Mishnah, other concerns than the challenge of Christianity and its reading of who is Israel predominated. Paul can find in the earliest documents of the Judaism that became normative no engaged interlocutors or partners in debate. His categories are not theirs, theirs are not his.

True, birth in Israel conferred advantages. But these remain to be specified; they cannot be assumed at the outset to fall into the category of the ethnic. The main point in the definition of Israel as sui generis lies not in its ethnic traits—for example, its politics, its alleged territoriality, its language, its customs and ceremonies and traditions and food preferences. What made Israel a unique society was its possession of the Torah. Israel in the model of the Torah from Heaven constituted Heaven's projection onto earth. Analysis of the traditions on earth corresponded to the discovery of the principles of creation; the full realization of the teachings of the Torah on earth, in the life of Israel, would transform Israel into a replica of heaven on earth.

What then of the salvation, so prominent an issue in Paul's thinking about Israel? It was an axiom of all forms of Judaism that, because Israel had sinned, it was punished by being given over into the hands of earthly empires; when it atoned, it was, and again would be, removed from their power. The means of atonement, reconciliation with God, were specified by the sages' system as the study of Torah, the practice of commandments, and the doing of good deeds. All human beings find a natural place within that account of the deepest structure of creation that the Torah sets forth. Thus, conforming to God's will and replicating heaven as a righteous, holy community, Israel would exercise the supernatural power of Torah. It would be able as a whole to do what some few saintly rabbis now could do. With access to supernatural power, redemption would naturally follow. At stake in this Judaism's Israel is God's stake in humanity.

The Judaism that focused its identity most fully in the Torah "found itself unable to separate ethnic identity from religious identity" (in Dunn's words) because, to begin with, the category *ethnic identity* bore no meaning whatsoever. It was Paul's category, fabricated for his theological purpose, meant to solve a problem particular to the system that he meant to shape. It was not the category of our sages of blessed memory, a fact that emerges as soon as we contemplate precisely how they understood their Israel. Over time, their meaning became the only meaning Israel would ever receive: holy people, and holy family or children of the patriarchs and matriarchs. To these meanings we now turn.

3

The Family of Israel

SURELY, *ISRAEL* STANDS for genealogy, and that is ethnic. For is not *Israel* in Judaism described as "the children of Israel," that is, the physical, genealogical heirs of Abraham, Isaac, Jacob, Sarah, Rebecca, Leah, and Rachel? Paul now moves over to the offensive: what greater mark of ethnicity can serve than the claim of common descent from the same ancestors? Judaism, with its confusion of genealogy and theology, its talk of its Israel as children of the patriarchs and matriarchs, its very appeal to *children* as the category modified by *of Israel,* surely forms the most ethnic of all religions. A social entity defined by a myth of common origin, language, territory—surely the religion of an *us* so defined is, and can only be, classified as ethnic. How do our sages respond?

Ethnic Israel: Genealogy and Endogamy as Indicators

Three indicators definitively classify a social entity as ethnic in genus: the importance assigned to genealogy, the doctrine of the entity's endogamy, and the view of the entity as forming a nation closed and bounded by genealogy and endogamy, and set aside or selected or sanctified by God. A social entity that imagines itself a single family (brothers and sisters) qualifies as ethnic. A social entity that insists marriages take place within that family is ethnic. And a social entity that calls itself chosen or elect in contrast to everybody else celebrates its ethnicity on the heights of heaven. It must follow that, by these indicators, Judaism's intransitive Israel—

Israel viewed on its own, and in relationship to not-Israel—surely belongs in the ethnic classification.

Substituting genealogy for theology and imposing endogamy as a primary demand, the Judaism of the dual Torah surely meets the definition of an ethnic religion. Therefore the claim that this Judaism conforms to the criteria of the ethnic religions hardly lays heavy demands on reason. And, as we will see in the next chapter, that same conception of Israel takes for granted the sanctity of the social entity. Any argument that rabbinic Judaism's Israel does not warrant classification as ethnic but as universal must address these formidable and established facts.

Judaism's Israel is portrayed as comprising persons who all descend from the same couple, Abraham and Sarah, and their immediate descendants. That is not merely a matter of myth; the child of a Jewish mother at birth forms Israel. Identity transmitted by birth is ethnic, not religious—surely Paul must challenge me, putting the entire matter in that single, ineluctable phrase *children of the flesh*. He is right: we are Israel by reason of birth into Israel. But is he right that we therefore must distinguish the flesh from the promise, the ethnic from the religious?

Rabbis do not agree. For along with the absolute given that the descendants of the holy family of the patriarchs and matriarchs should intramarry or practice perfect endogamy, there is another, disorienting and qualifying fact: the convert becomes wholly, completely, Israel—without differentiation by reason of his or her ethnic past. So the datum that a place in Israel is conferred merely by birth is matched by the conception that the convert, who accepts the yoke of Heaven and the yoke of the Torah and commandments, has a future but no past genealogy; a convert's estate may be plundered by Israelites, his wife and children of the period before his conversion having no familial relationship with him, therefore no rights of natural inheritance. What he loses on the one side, he gains on the other: his rightful place in Israel, the ethnic as much as the theological entity. There is no distinguishing the one from the other, since the ethnic dimension simply takes the measure in the here and now of the theological conviction.

Conversion defies ethnicity, because it ignores the very givens of the ethnic identity. No dimension of the ethnic dimension of a social entity exceeds in reach the conception that the ethnic group, joined by a common language, a territorial aspiration, and a way of life, also forms a family. But if I join the family by an act of faith and an accompanying rite to express the faith, then family does not mean here what it ordinarily means; it becomes a supernatural, not a natural, category.

Family defines a vivid and compelling metaphor for the social entity, claiming that persons lacking immediate relationships are children of the same forebears. The metaphor of a group as family takes shape in two matters: first, the invention of a common genealogy; second, the promulgation of strict endogamy. Certainly, the Judaism of the dual Torah presents itself as ethnic in these two matters; it posits a common ancestry for its Israel. Its Israel is also conceived as perfectly endogamous. It follows that the Judaism of the dual Torah sets forth a doctrine of Israel that conforms in good and substantial ways to the minimum definition of an ethnic doctrine of a social entity.

Much depends, however, on how we interpret the allegations that Israel defines itself genealogically rather than theologically. A genealogy in this-worldly terms may transmit itself through marriage (e.g., one marries into the family). This one does not. The marriage of a Jew to an unconverted gentile does not affect the status of the gentile, who is not absorbed into the family. If the gentile is a female, the offspring are gentile; if male, the offspring belong to Israel, enjoying the status of the mother, but the father remains an outsider. On the other hand, the act of conversion confers upon the gentile the status of Israelite, equal, as we have seen, to any other Israelite. That means that a genealogy the gentile otherwise cannot claim is conferred on the gentile through an act of faith (baptism for women, baptism and circumcision for men). Imputing parenthood of the gentile to Abraham and Sarah, as is made explicit in the liturgy of the synagogue when the former gentile is called to the Torah by his or her Hebrew name as "son or daughter of our father Abraham," tells the entire tale.

What that fact indicates is simple. The appeal to genealogy forms a step in the metaphorization of the social entity into Israel. It radically transforms an ethnic metaphor of genealogy, turning family into a theological statement of status. To state matters more simply, if a convert is given genealogy within Israel, as he or she is, it is a mythic genealogy, not a natural one, and the transformation of the outsider into the insider takes place on terms no less supernatural than that conceived by Paul as the result of faith. In both cases, what happens by reason of faith is a change in the status of the person vis-à-vis the social entity. This change pertains solely to matters of conviction, entirely in line, in the case of rabbinic Judaism, with the definition of Israel as those who enjoy a portion in the world to come by reason of origin in Israel and acceptance of the doctrinal indicators of belonging to Israel.

Why suppose otherwise? The reason people commonly conceive Judaism to appeal to genealogy, not theology, in its definition of Israel is not difficult to identify. Rabbinic Judaism lays heavy emphasis on a metaphor of genealogy, involving family and marriage. Reifying the metaphor is a quite natural error. The error consists in treating as natural and this-worldly the remarkable fact that through an act of spirituality—conversion in matters of conviction and consequent conduct—a gentile may join the family. The metaphor of Israel as extended family thus makes a theological statement in a theological context.

How and Why Judaism's Israel Is Set Forth as a Family

To understand what is meant by the genealogical metaphor so characteristic of rabbinic Judaism, we have to identify the context in which that metaphor gains prominence. In the documents of the dual Torah, the formulation of the theory of Israel as an extended family comes to prominence in the writings of 400–600 c.e. These writings came to closure after Christianity became the state religion of Rome, and, at salient points, they address questions important to the Christian polemic against Judaism framed in the aftermath of that transforming event.[1] Specifically, by claiming that Israel constituted the actual, living, present family of Abraham and Sarah, Isaac and Rebecca, Jacob and Leah and Rachel, the sages met head-on the Christian claim that there was—or could ever be—some other Israel and that the existing Jews no longer constituted Israel. The metaphor given prominence in the late fourth- and fifth-century sages' writings formed a remarkable counterpoint to the allegation that Israel after the flesh has been rejected by God and that the Jews of the present time and place bear no lineage to biblical Israel, now realized in Christianity.

The metaphor of the family proved pointed. The sages framed their idea of Israel within the metaphor of genealogy because, facing the claim that there was an Israel other than the existing one they knew, they appealed to the fleshly connection, the family, as the rationale for Israel's social existence. Christianity's political polemic against the existing Israel as illegitimate—children of the flesh, not children of the promise, in contradiction to Paul's subtle formulation of matters three centuries earlier—made necessary the contrary allegation, appealing to a genealogy that was at once physical, for Jews by birth, and theological, for converts.

Not only so, but the metaphor permitted the sages to cast in a plausible way the world-historical events set forth by the politics of a Christian Rome. Using the metaphor of a family beginning with Abraham, Isaac, and Jacob, Israel could best sort out its relationships with the nations, meaning Christian Rome in particular, by drawing into the family other social entities with which it found it had to relate. So Rome became the brother. That affinity came to light only in writings that reached closure well after the legitimation of Christianity and the conversion of the ruling household to that faith. The metaphor of the family dealt with the facts of the situation: Christian Rome shared with Israel the common patrimony of Scripture—and said so. Documents held to have reached closure prior to Constantine's conversion know nothing of Rome as brother, and impute little use to the genealogical metaphor. Those that were concluded afterward invariably play heavily upon that theme.

The character of the sages' thought on Israel therefore proved remarkably congruent to the conditions of public discourse that confronted them. But the implications of these facts for our issue should not be missed. The conception that *family* is by nature an ethnic metaphor is contradicted by both Christian and Judaic insistence that *family* is subject to supernatural intervention. This reaches expression in a variety of ways. The simplest is the conception that, within the Torah's family, natural relationships are transformed. The sage takes priority over the natural father, just as Jesus

Christ takes priority over the natural father. The sage's imputed genealogy, like the convert's imputed genealogy, is no more ethnic than the church's claim that Jesus Christ recasts the conception of family. In both cases, *family* becomes a metaphor for a supernatural reality.

The Theological Meaning of the Genealogical Metaphor

When the fourth-century sages wished to know what (an) Israel was, they reread the scriptural story Israel's origins to find the answer. To begin with, as Scripture told them the story, Israel was a man, Jacob, and his children (and by extension his descendants) through various wives and concubines are the children of Jacob. That man's name was also Israel, and, it followed that the children of Israel comprised his extended family. So Israel formed the family of Abraham and Sarah, Isaac and Rebecca, Jacob and Leah and Rachel. The conception of the social entity represented by the category *Israel* therefore invoked the metaphor of genealogy to explain the bonds that linked persons unseen into a single social entity; the shared traits were imputed, not empirical. That social metaphor of Israel—a simple one, really, and easily grasped—bore consequences in two ways.

First, children in general are admonished to follow the good example of their parents. The deeds of the patriarchs and matriarchs therefore taught lessons on how the children were to act. Second, of greater interest in an account of Israel as a social metaphor, is that "Israel" lived twice, once in the patriarchs and matriarchs, a second time in the life of the heirs, as the descendants relived those earlier lives. The stories of the family were carefully reread to provide a picture of the meaning of the latter-day events of the descendants of that same family. Accordingly, the lives of the patriarchs signaled the history of Israel. The former may be represented in a limited, ethnic framework. The latter cannot. Once the lives of the patriarchs and matriarchs stand for the future history of their descendants, we move far from a narrowly ethnic conception of genealogy; now the patriarchs and matriarchs are transformed into paradigms of social being.[2]

Genealogy is made to serve as a principal medium for theological discourse. It is no more to be read in a literal and this-worldly way than the conception of the church as the mystical body of Christ is to be read in such a way; that is, the metaphor simply does not work when removed from its setting of transcendence. Judaism is no more ethnic than Christianity.

For the comparison of the two supernatural entities, church and Israel, each expressed through its manifestly fleshly metaphor, is exact and fits the very specific occasion. The polemical purpose of the claim that the abstraction Israel was to be compared to the family of the mythic ancestor lies right at the surface. With another Israel, the Christian church, now claiming to constitute the true one, the sages found it possible to confront that claim and to turn it against the other side. "You claim to form Israel after the spirit. Fine, and we are Israel after the flesh—and genealogy forms the link, that alone."[3] That fleshly continuity formed of all of us a single family, rendering spurious the notion that Israel could be other than genealogically defined.

"Israel" as an Extended Family in the Mishnah

While one influential scriptural myth of Israel treats the social entity as an extended family, the Mishnah's authorship rarely makes use of that sense of the category. Like Israel sui generis, the meaning of Israel as family always bears supernatural, not narrowly familial or genealogical, meaning or it occurs in a liturgical context, which is the same thing. When *fathers* or *ancestors* is joined to the noun Israel, a supernatural sense intrudes; for example, "God of the fathers of Israel" (M. Bik. 1:4) and "All Israelites are sons of princes" (which is ordinarily understood to allude to their being children of Abraham) (M. Shab. 14:4). Not every genealogical reference demands the sense of family at all—"the children of Israel" (M. Neg. 2:1), for example, is simply synonymous with Israel the social entity. These usages are not commonplace and play no role in the formulation of the law, to which the bulk of the Mishnah is devoted. In all, we look in vain in the Mishnah, Tosefta, Sifra, and the two Sifrés for an extensive development of the conception of Israel as an extended family, heir in the latter days to the merit piled up in heaven by Abraham, Isaac, Jacob, Sarah, Rebecca, Leah, and Rachel.

Can we say that the Mishnaic phase had presented an encompassing theory of society as a whole? In general terms, yes, but in specifics, no. Invoking the metaphor *Israel* for a group subjected to metaphor and so identified with the biblical Israel, the Mishnah accounted for the whole. As to the parts, the here and the now of household and village, the Mishnah's Israel accomplished a suitable explanation. But the space between the theoretical and the mundane was left vacant. By *Israel,* the Mishnah's system had explained the identification of that large entity, the entirety of the social group, with biblical Israel. In its extraordinary exegesis of the everyday as model of the sacred, this system had also infused in the parts that sense that the whole was meant to make. But the parts remained just that: details of a larger whole that derived place and proportion only in that whole. That abstraction of Israel left the middle-range components of society unaccounted for.

The Mishnah could explain village and all Israel, just as its system used the word *Israel* for individual and entire social entity. But the region and its counterparts, the *we* composed of regions, the corporate society of the Jews of a given country, language group, or the like—these did not constitute subdivisions of the Israel that knew all and each, but nothing in between. The omitted entity, I see, was the family itself, which played no important role in the Mishnah's system, except as one of the taxonomic indicators. In contrast, Israel as family imparted to the details an autonomy and a meaning of their own, *so that each complex component of the whole formed a microcosm of the whole: family to village to Israel as one large family.*

The village then comprised Israel, as much as did the region, the neighborhood, and the corporate society that people could empirically identify, and the theoretical social entity they could only imagine—all formed all Israel, viewed under the aspect of Heaven. Of still greater consequence, each household—that is, each building block of the village community—constituted in itself a model of and for Israel. Dealing with exquisite detail and the intangible whole, the Mishnah's system had left that realm of the society of Jews in the workaday household and village outside the metaphorical frame of Israel; Israel viewed in the image of family made up that omitted middle range.

That theory of Israel as a society made up of persons who because they constituted a family stood in a clear relationship of obligation and responsibility to one another corresponded to what people much later would call the social contract. The web of interaction now was spun not from the gossamer thread of abstraction and theory but from the tough hemp of family ties. Israel formed a society because Israel was compared to an extended family. That, sum and substance, supplied to the Jews in their households (themselves a made-up category that, in the end, transformed the relationship of the nuclear family into an abstraction capable of holding together quite unrelated persons) an account of the tie from household to household, from village to village, encompassing, ultimately, all Israel.

Now if we ask the authorship of the Mishnah to point to its encompassing theory of Israel as an ongoing society, where will they lead us? If they tell us that Israel forms a society because it is not not-Israel, they evade the question altogether. For not-Israel formed an undifferentiated other. It did not constitute a society, but only a category. For the same reason Israel as caste contained no elements that could be spun out into a theory of interpersonal relationships that would account for the ongoing life of households in communities, villages, towns, and so on. The theory of society that infuses the Mishnaic system forms part of a larger abstract program: Israel constitutes a holy people, a people apart, a people different from all other peoples; Israel constitutes a caste. But how everyday Israel forms a community, how in the aggregate everyday relationships are composed and held together, and how to account for the corresponding middle-range aggregates of not-Israel—these are not questions answered by the Mishnah's metaphors for Israel.

If we form a family, then we know full well what links us: the common ancestry, the obligations imposed by common ancestry on the cousins who make up the family today. The link between the commonplace interactions and relationships that make us into a community, on the one side, and that encompassing entity, Israel, on the other, now is drawn. The large comprehends the little, the abstraction of us overall (the circumcised, for instance) gains concrete reality in the us of the here and now of home and village, all forming a family. In that fundamental way, the metaphor of Israel as family therefore provided the field theory of Israel, linking the most abstract component, the entirety of the social group, to the most mundane, the specificity of the household. Again, the metaphor of family offered an encompassing theory of society, an account of the social contract encompassing all social entities that no other metaphor accomplished.

The relevance of these observations to our governing issue can now be specified. A further appreciation for the theological, as against the ethnic, context in which the genealogical metaphor is to be interpreted derives from a richer understanding of the conclusions the sages drew from the metaphor. These were not exclusionary, except in religious terms; true, the outsider was not a member of the family or the tribe, but by an act of religious character he or she could become one. But the metaphor served not only to define boundaries and to provide a map for crossing frontiers. The metaphor of Israel as family supplied an encompassing theory of society, accounting for that sense of Israel constituting a corporate social entity that clearly infused the documents of the Judaism of the dual Torah from the very outset.

Such a theory explained not only who Israel was a whole. It also set forth the responsibilities of Israel's social entity, its society; it defined the character of that entity, explaining who owes what to whom and why; and it accounted for the inner structure and interplay of relationships within the community, here and now, constituted by Jews in their villages and neighborhoods of towns. Accordingly, Israel as family bridged the gap between an account of the entirety of the social group, Israel, and the components of that social group as they lived out their lives in their households and villages. From Israel viewed as an extended family came an encompassing theory of society, covering all components from least to greatest, holding the whole together in correct order and proportion.

Israel as Family: The Patriarchs and Matriarchs and the Family of Israel

Families inherited the estate of the founders, and Israel was a family with a sizable heritage and inheritance. Thinking not in terms of abstractions but in personal and concrete ways, the sages, through what they said about personalities of Scripture, were able to make perfectly clear statements for themselves. Along these same lines, when the church theologians and historians faced the task of explaining the connection between diverse nations or peoples and the church, they worked out relationships between the king of a country and Jesus. The correspondence between Jesus and Abgar, which accounted for the place of the Church of Edessa within the family of Christianity, is one example. Because the church understood that not only Jesus' blood relatives but also his disciples (standing in a supernatural relationship with him) entered into the original communion, the invented discipleship of kings made a place, within a larger social theory of the church, for the new and diverse groups. When, in the fourth century, a principal world ruler did convert, the church had an understanding of the role of persons and personalities in the history of salvation. The mode of thought before us, therefore, finds ample place in a larger scheme of thinking about society and the relationships of its components. Once more, it is clear, if Israel is ethnic, so is Christ, and in the same terms and for the same purposes of formulation and articulation of a theology.

Families have histories, and Israel as family found in the record of its family history those points of coherence that transformed events into meaningful patterns, that is, into the history of the social unit. The sages looked at the facts of history to find the laws of history. They proposed to generalize and, out of generalization, to explain their own particular circumstance. Genesis provided facts concerning the family. Careful sifting of those facts will yield the laws that dictated why to that family things happened one way, rather than some other. Among these social laws of the family history, one type took priority: the laws that explained the rise and fall of empires and pointed toward the ultimate end of it all. Scripture provided the model for the ages of empires, yielding a picture of four monarchies, to be followed by Israel as the fifth. In reading Genesis, in particular, the sages found that time and again events in the lives of the patriarchs prefigured the four monarchies, among which the fourth, last, and most intolerable, of course, was Rome. Israel's history falls under God's dominion. Whatever will happen carries out God's plan, and that plan for the future has been laid out in the account of the origins supplied by Genesis. The fourth kingdom, Rome, is part of that plan, which we can discover by carefully studying Abraham's life and God's word to him:

Genesis Rabbah XLIV:XVIII

1. A. "Then the Lord said to Abram, 'Know of a surety [that your descendants will be sojourners in a land that is not theirs, and they will be slaves there, and they will be oppressed for four hundred years; but I will bring judgment on the nation which they serve, and afterward they shall come out with great possessions']" (Gen. 15:13–14):

B. "Know" that I shall scatter them.

C. "Of a certainty" that I shall bring them back together again.

D. "Know" that I shall put them out as a pledge [in expiation of their sins].

E. "Of a certainty" that I shall redeem them.

F. "Know" that I shall make them slaves.

G. "Of a certainty" that I shall free them.

This passage parses the cited verse and joins within its simple formula the entire history of Israel, punishment and forgiveness alike. Not only the patriarchs, but also the matriarchs, so acted as to shape the future life of the family, Israel.

Everything that Abraham did brought a reward to his descendants. The enormous emphasis on the way in which Abraham's deeds prefigured the history of Israel—in the wilderness and in the land, and, finally, in the age to come—provokes us to wonder who held that there were other children of Abraham, besides this Israel. One answer is clear: the triumphant Christians in particular, who right from the beginning, with Paul and the evangelists, claimed that they were a new Israel and said this in so many words. Obviously, it is the merit of the ancestors that connects the living Israel to the lives of the patriarchs and matriarchs of old.

While Abraham founded Israel, Isaac and Jacob carried forth the birthright and the blessing. This they did through the process of selection, ending in the assignment of the birthright to Jacob alone. The importance of that fact for the definition of Israel hardly requires explication. The lives of all three patriarchs flowed together, each being identified with the other as a single long life. This immediately produced the proposition that the historical life of Israel, the nation, continued the individual lives of the patriarchs. The theory of who is Israel, therefore, is seen once more to have rested on genealogy: Israel is one extended family, all being children of the same fathers and mothers, the patriarchs and matriarchs of Genesis. This theory of Israelite society and of the Jewish people at the time of the sages of Genesis Rabbah made of the people a family, and of genealogy, a kind of ecclesiology. The importance of that proposition in countering the Christian claim to be a new Israel cannot escape notice. Israel, the sages maintained, is Israel after the flesh, and that in a most literal sense. But the basic claim, for its part, depended upon the facts of Scripture, not upon the logical requirements of theological dispute. Here is how those facts emerged in the case of Isaac.

The importance of Isaac in particular derived from his relationship to the two nations that would engage in struggle: Jacob, who was and is Israel, and Esau, who stood for Rome. By himself, as a symbol for Israel's history, Isaac remained a shadowy figure. Still, Isaac plays his role in setting forth the laws of Israel's history; Esau, in the sages' typology, always stands for Rome. Esau is not an outsider—not a gentile—but also not Israel, the legitimate heir. We once more recall the power of the social theory to hold together all of the middle-range components of society: all nations within a single theory.

Israel and Rome—these two contend for the world. Still, Isaac plays his part in the matter. Rome does have a legitimate claim, and that claim demands recognition—an amazing, if grudging concession on the part of the sages that Christian Rome at least is Esau, different from the gentiles, but also not Israel.

Every detail of the narrative of Genesis served to prefigure what was to be, and Israel as extended family found itself, time and again, in the revealed facts of the family record of Abraham, Isaac, and Israel. We see how the sages thought and therefore understood the positions they reached. Imagining the group to constitute a family, they organized the entire social world—Israel's part, the nations' share—within the single metaphor at hand. That mode of thought gave them a rich resource for interpreting the everyday history of

Israel in the context of world politics and also for explaining the future of Israel.

Israel as Family (2): Merit in Genesis Rabbah

In documents that reached closure in the century after Constantine's legalization of Christianity and its progressive establishment as the state religion, the doctrine of merit joined with the notion of Israel as children of Israel to give concrete substance to the explanation of what and who Israel was. Within the metaphor invoked, also, by the notion of the *zekhut abot,* the merit of the ancestors, Israel was a family, the children of Abraham, Isaac, and Jacob. Israel hence fell into the genus *family* as the particular species of family generated by Abraham and Sarah. The distinguishing trait of that species was that it possessed the inheritance, or heritage, of the patriarchs and matriarchs, and that inheritance, consisting of merit, served the descendants and heirs as protection and support. Here once again, we find a metaphor drawn from ethnic life transformed into a supernatural statement concerning an enchanted community, a family in an other-worldly sense.

The metaphor of family thus worked itself out within its own logic, generating secondary analogies and comparisons. The most important of these involved the analogy of spiritual and material estates, a theory which took up the rather general notion of merit, which surely existed as a potentiality, we noted, in the Mishnah. Merit was joined to the metaphor of the genealogy of patriarchs and matriarchs and served to form the missing link, explaining how the inheritance and heritage were transmitted from them to their heirs. Consequently, the family, Israel, could draw upon the family estate, consisting of the inherited merit of matriarchs and patriarchs, in such a way as to benefit today from the heritage of yesterday. This notion involved very concrete problems. If Israel, the family sinned, it could call on the merit accumulated by Abraham and Isaac at the binding of Isaac (Genesis 22) to win forgiveness for that sin. True, "fathers will not die on account of the sin of the sons," but the children may benefit from the merit of their forebears. That concrete expression of the larger metaphor imparted to the metaphor a practical consequence, moral and theological, that was not at all neglected.

The doctrine of the inherited merit of the ancestors served as a component of the powerful polemic concerning Israel. Like the metaphor of which it forms a part, it is both genealogical and not at all limited by considerations of race or ethnic inheritance. It speaks about family, but in dimensions of an entirely spiritual character, since the source of *zekhut abot* is an act to which God responds, and the mode of transmission is God's capacity to remember on behalf of one's descendants the remarkable and evocative deeds of a prior generation. It is a deeply spiritual concept given a fleshly formulation for reasons of context.

Specifically, that concrete, historical Israel in the literature before us manifestly and explicitly claimed fleshly origin in Abraham and Sarah. The extended family indeed constituted precisely what the Christian theologians said it did: an Israel after the flesh, a family linked by genealogy. The heritage then became an inheritance, and what was inherited from the ancestors was a heavenly store, a treasure of merit, which protected the descendants when their own merit proved insufficient. A survey of Genesis Rabbah indicates the character and use of the doctrine of merit, because that systematic reading of the book of Genesis dealt with the founders of the family and made explicit the definition of Israel as family. We will see that merit draws in its wake the notion of the inheritance of an ongoing family, that of Abraham and Sarah, and merit worked itself out in the moments of crisis of that family in its larger affairs.

In the first example we see a definition of merit and how it is attained. It may be personal or inherited. Here it is personal. Specifically, Jacob reflects on the power that Esau's merit had gained for Esau. He had gained that merit by living in the land of Israel and also by paying honor and respect to Isaac. Jacob then feared that, because of the merit gained by Esau, he, Jacob, would not be able to overcome him. So merit worked on its own; it was a credit gained by proper action, which went to the credit of the person who had done that action.

Genesis Rabbah LXXVI:II

2. A. "Then Jacob was greatly afraid and distressed" (Gen. 32:7): [This is Jacob's soliloquy:] "Because of all those years that

Esau was living in the Land of Israel, perhaps he may come against me with the power of the merit he has now attained by dwelling in the Land of Israel.

B. "Because of all those years of paying honor to his father, perhaps he may come against me with the power of the merit he attained by honoring his father.

C. "So he said: 'Let the days of mourning for my father be at hand, then I will slay my brother Jacob' (Gen. 27:41).

D. "Now the old man is dead."

E. Said R. Judah bar Simon, "This is what the Holy One, blessed be he, had said to him, 'Return to the land of your fathers and to your kindred' (Gen. 31:3). [Supplying a further soliloquy for Jacob:] 'Perhaps the stipulations [of protection by God] applied only up to this point [at which I enter the land].'"

We see that merit is not only inherited but attained, and the source of the merit may be simply dwelling in the land of Israel itself. The very physical location of a human being within the land infuses that person with merit; the land, as much as the ancestors, is a generative source. From our perspective, however, Israel as family makes the patriarchs and matriarchs the key to merit. Another important side of the conception of merit attributes to the ancestors that store of merit on which the descendants draw. So the Israelites later on enjoy enormous merit through the deeds of the patriarchs and matriarchs. That conception comes to expression in what follows:

Genesis Rabbah LXXVI:V

2. A. " . . . for with only my staff I crossed this Jordan, and now I have become two companies:"

B. R. Judah bar Simon in the name of R. Yohanan: "In the Torah, in the Prophets, and in the Writings we find proof that the Israelites were able to cross the Jordan only on account of the merit achieved by Jacob:

C. "In the Torah: ' . . . for with only my staff I crossed this Jordan, and now I have become two companies.'

D. "In the prophets: 'Then you shall let your children know, saying, "Israel came over this Jordan on dry land"'" (Josh. 4:22), meaning our father, Israel.

E. "In the Writings: 'What ails you, O you sea, that you flee?

You Jordan, that you turn backward? At the presence of the God of Jacob' (Ps. 114:5ff)."

F. Said R. Levi, "There is a place, where the Jordan falls with a roar into the hot springs of Tiberias.

G. "In his fear Jacob hid in there and locked Esau out. But the Holy One, blessed be he, dug a hole for him at another spot. 'When you pass through the waters, I will be with you, and through the rivers, and they shall not overflow you, when you walk through the fire, you shall not be burned' (Isa. 43:2)."

A narrowly ethnic system will formulate rules that apply only to its social entity, and, when the rules concern genealogy, an ethnic Judaism certainly would make no provision whatever for gentiles to participate in the system's processes. But here we have gentiles who inherit the merit of their ancestors too. The Egyptians gained merit by honoring Jacob in his death. This same point then registers for the Canaanites. The connection is somewhat farfetched—that is, through the reference to the threshing floor—but the point is a strong one. Yet merit derives not only from exceptional deeds of a religious or moral character. People attain merit simply through hard work, through living up to their calling.

The picture is clear. Israel constitutes a family as a genealogical and juridical fact. It inherits the estate of the ancestors. It hands on that estate. It lives by the example of the matriarchs and patriarchs, and its history exemplifies events in their lives. The governing law is that Israel constitutes a family and inherits the merit laid up by the ancestors as a treasure for the descendants.

Genealogy as a Theological Metaphor

Once the sages had defined the social entity of Israel by analogy with a family, they naturally imposed the same metaphor on other social entities. By its nature, the metaphor is inclusive, not exclusive. It is the other-than-ethnic, universal character of the metaphor of family that serves to encompass all other social entities within a single field of analysis. That instrument of thought therefore allowed the sages to explain within a single, unitary theory what happened to Israel and to everyone else that mattered. A brief account of the outcome of extending the same metaphor suffices. If

Abraham, Isaac, and Jacob stand for Israel later on, then Ishmael, Edom, and Esau represent Rome. Hence whatever the sages found out about those figures told them something about Rome and its character, history, and destiny. God has unconditionally promised to redeem Israel, but if Israel repents, then the redemption will come with greater glory. The challenge of Christianity from the beginning had come from its spiritualization of Israel, expressed in Paul's profound reflections at Romans 9–11, but contained also in the distinction between the spirit and the flesh in the definition of Israel. Here, as we have now seen, that challenge finds its answer in its opposite and counterpart: the utter and complete "genealogization" of Israel.

To state matters negatively, the people could no more conceive that they were not the daughters and sons of their fathers and mothers than that they were not one large family, the family of Abraham, Isaac, and Jacob, Israel after the flesh. The powerful stress on the enduring merit of the patriarchs and matriarchs, the social theory that treated Israel as one large, extended family, the actual children of Abraham, Isaac, and Jacob—these now-familiar metaphors for the fleshly continuity met head-on the contrary position framed by Paul and restated by Christian theologians from his time onward. But the metaphor of family for Judaism's Israel proved remarkably apt for the requirements of the new era, and that is why the potential metaphor came to realization in just this age. In the uses to which the sages in Genesis Rabbah put the metaphor, we see the impact of those requirements.

The metaphor of the family served to bring within the shelter of a single encompassing theory all of the components of that society, Israel, covered by the abstraction at hand. *Family* explained the composition of the household, an economic unit of production. *Family* accounted for the interrelationships of households of a certain sort—the Jewish sort—in a mixed village or in a village made up of only Jewish households. *Family* allowed Jews to relate their own social entity to those other entities the political presence of which they chose to take account. In all, the power of the metaphor lay in its possibility of joining all social entities—whether groups, classes, or another order altogether—into a single and uniform entity: the families of humanity, whether of Israel or of Esau.

But the power of the metaphor also contained its pathos. *Family*—whether Israel, whether Esau—left Israel different but not at all singular; Balaam's curse that brought blessing, "A people that dwells apart," has yet to take effect. The genealogical metaphor accomplished the opposite of setting forth a narrowly ethnic theory of Israel.

Then what about the other powerful metaphor, Israel as the chosen people or nation? We next turn to the formulation of Israel that has struck the world as most particular and least universal in its sense, imparting to the Judaism that defines that Israel the status of a narrowly ethnic religion.

4

The People of Israel and How They Know God

PAUL NOW TURNS to the third way in which Israel after the flesh has always defined itself: as a people or a nation. "Do you not claim to be the chosen people? Are we not debating about who, beyond Israelites by birth, is chosen? Surely the very terms of the argument we are having define matters my way: ethnic group, spiritual community!"

The challenge compels response. Surely Paul is right in distinguishing the ethnic from the religious, the flesh from the promise. A religion assigned to a single nation is a national religion; a religion that belongs to a single ethnic group is an ethnic religion. However we define nation and people, the upshot is the same. The Jews by definition are a people of one religion;[1] Judaism then must be a religion of one people. How then is Judaism not ethnic? Paul asks. No wonder, Paul concludes, it is necessary to distinguish the ethnic religion from the universal religion! Otherwise, where will the gentiles find a place at Sinai and a share in the God of Abraham, Isaac, Jacob, Sarah, Rebecca, Leah and Rachel? They are, by definition, not Israelites by birth, but in Judaism's view, Israelites by birth are all there are.

What Is at Stake in the Election of Israel?

Because Scripture uses such words as *nation* and *people,* it follows that if Israel is not an ethnic group like any other or a family in any this-worldly sense of the word, then does its nationhood or peoplehood correspond to that of any other group? Here we come to the crux of the characterization of Israel as ethnic. Is not the term *the chosen people* the supreme indicator of ethnicity in religion? To answer that question in documentary context, we have to find out in what way this Judaism actually defines the category *people*, or *nation*, in which it classifies its Israel. When we know how the election of Israel shapes the definition of Israel, we will take the penultimate step toward the concluding question of our work: In what way does this people or nation relate to God, by whom—the Torah insists— this nation is known, elected, and especially beloved? The answer to that question spells out the character of this peculiar people, the very particular nation that appeals to the Torah to explain its existence: Is God our God alone? How does God become manifest here on earth? An ethnic religion answers, We alone possess the answer to that question. Judaism's answer, as we will see, invites into Israel all of humanity, without differentiation in regard to race, national origin, or previous condition of servitude.

When we know what is at stake in Israel's election, we may come to a final solution to the riddle of the ethnicity of this Judaism's Israel. The stakes are purely theological. When the sages spoke of Israel in the context of election, they had in mind precisely what Christianity conceived the church to comprise, broadly construed: the locus in this world for the presence of God. The people or nation, Israel, was not only a supernatural family, sui generis; it also was a people or nation, sui generis. What made the group distinctive found its definition in God's purpose in creating the world. Israel on its own bore no importance whatsoever; Israel within God's plan, living in accord with that plan, formed God's stake in this world.

The definition of Israel offered by the Judaism described here not only left no space for an ethnic Israel. It also comprehended the world of peoples and nations only under the aspect of eternity, therefore defining Israel's peoplehood solely and uniquely by appeal to God's purpose. In the sense in which Rome was an empire or Egypt a nation and a people, Israel found no elements of a plausible definition; Israel's paradigmatic story set Israel as counterpart to Rome, defined Israel by appeal to its Exodus from Egypt, always and only in consequence of God's intervention into human affairs.

This language, for the Christian faithful, surely resonates with the language that speaks of Jesus Christ as God incarnate. God is no more incarnate in a human being like any other than God elects a nation by selection among nations of the same genus. Jesus Christ for Christianity—for Paul's Christianity—is unique and beyond all comparison to other human beings. Israel in our sages' Judaism is unique and defined in its own genus, not in the genus of other ethnic or national groups at all.

That is the sole conclusion to be drawn from the formulations we have already examined, with Israel as the holy family, its patriarchs and matriarchs as paradigms of its history. But the same fundamental fact comes to striking expression in a still more compelling way when sages say in so many words that Israel formed that locus in the world in which God's presence came to rest. In Torah study, Israel's sages prepare the way for prophecy. Israel forms God's domain on earth. The vision of an Israel that takes shape around synagogues and schools carries us deep into this Judaism's understanding of Israel as God's unique people. That definition then forms part of a larger public conception of Israel within the metaphor of a God who takes up residence within a social group.

To our sages, God is always God, everywhere God, uniquely God: creator of heaven and earth. To our sages, Adam and Eve (that is, all humanity) are created "in our image, after our likeness." Israel, within humanity, aspires to make a place for God within creation. Christianity will understand that aspiration when it recognizes that God incarnate and the language invented here for Ahaz represent the same definition of matters. Through Jesus Christ, God became a man and walked among us, so Paul, with all Christianity, affirms. Ahaz speaks for our sages' Israel: "If there are no children, there will be no adults. If there are no adults, there will be no disciples. If there are no disciples, there will be no sages. If there are no sages, there will be no prophets. If there are no prophets, the Holy One, blessed be he, will not allow his presence to come to rest in the world." If Christianity's God incarnate is to be distinguished from God's presence coming to rest in the world, I do not know how to differentiate the sense of the one from the intent of the other.

Incarnation and election address the same deeply scriptural aspiration: to encounter, know, serve, and love God.

The ethnic formulation of matters becomes possible only when Israel's Torah is disregarded, Israel's sages dismissed, Israel's sanctity reduced to its this-worldly trivialities of politics and ethnic preferences. If Israel is elect, then God is the God of Israel—and of all who come under the wings of God's presence by entering into Israel. The secular language *Israel's way of life* shows us how any ethnic formulation of matters begins in the complete rejection of the Judaism that anybody purports to describe. It is not Israel's way of life—a collection of customs and ceremonies, food preferences and shared sentimentality about minor-mode singing—but God's commandments. It is not our civilization, but God's kingdom. God's people is Israel, because God's people comprises all who have accepted God's Torah and commandments, without regard to ethnic origin. Israel is not holier than anyone else; there is no scale of sanctification. Israel alone is holy, because God alone is God.

Once more, in the rabbinic context, we find no space or place for the category of the ethnic. Were Israel particular, gentiles would find no equal place, but even slaves entered Israel at the moment of their acquisition and circumcision (in the case of males) or baptism (males and females alike). Converts have no past, no relationships of any kind; they come from no ethnic group and they do not transfer into an ethnic group. That judgment applied equally to slaves, Roman emperors, and Greek philosophers. They come from nowhere, when they enter holy Israel. There is no gentile nor Jew, but only supernatural, holy Israel.

The sages' response to the ethnic formulation of Israel can only be God is God, not ours, not yours. Our way of life is not ours. God has commanded that way of life, sanctifying us by the commandments, through the Torah. It is not God's people—which we comprise—that forms an exclusive channel of divine grace. It is God who takes up a presence where God's word lives. Israel is not elect because God chose Israel. Israel is elect because the Torah defines Israel, and the Torah is the medium of God's grace to humanity. Israel is Adam's counterpart, just as Christ, for Christianity, is Adam's counterpart. The Torah is not the source of the knowledge of sin but its antidote, calling into being the covenant between

God and Israel at Sinai, the counterpart and opposite of Adam in Eden.

The People of Israel in the Mishnah

When the framers of the Mishnah use the word *Israel,* they may well mean "the people of God," "your people," and the like. In that usage, *Israel* refers to a supernatural social entity, one that stands in a special relationship with God and addresses God in distinctive terms. Like the reference to Israel as sui generis, such nongeneric usages, as I have already suggested, most commonly occur in liturgical settings, for example, "Save, O Lord, your people, the remnant of Israel" (M. Ber. 4:4) and "Let us bless the Lord, our God, the God of Israel" (M. Ber. 7:3). In relationship to God, Israel always bears a supernatural dimension; for example, "So too, the Holy One, blessed be he, purifies Israel" (M. Yoma 8:9) and "The Holy One, blessed be he, found as a utensil to hold a blessing for Israel only peace" (M. Uqs. 3:12).

Rightly understood, the supernatural dimensions and considerations pertinent to this Israel indeed encompass the bulk of the rules of the Mishnah, even where the word *Israel* is not used. Where *Israel* serves as antonym for *gentile,* the sense, even when neutral, bears subterranean meaning of a supernatural order. For example, "An Israelite may not raise pigs in any location" (M. San. 7:7), a rule that bears the sense "but a gentile may do so" carries no explicit explanation. But the implicit sense—that the gentile is not subject to those rules of heaven that make Israel what it is— everywhere prevails. Along these same lines, the rule that "An Israelite may lend at usury the capital of a gentile with the gentile's knowledge and consent" (M. B.M. 5:6) stands for a more than merely an ethnic difference.

The sense of Israel as a people in close relationship to God occurs in Tosefta as in the Mishnah, in liturgical contexts most commonly: "Listen to the sound of the prayer of your people, Israel" (T. Ber. 3:7). Israel's "father in heaven" occurs at T. Shab. 14:5, Sifra Qedoshim 10:8: " . . . which bring peace between Israel and their father in heaven." The inclusion of the word Israel in all liturgies bears this same supernatural connotation, as in " . . . who sanctifies the Sabbath, Israel, and the seasons" (T. Ber. 3:13). Explicit statements on the supernatural status of Israel include the following: "Beloved are Israel, for even though they are unclean, the Presence of God is yet among them" (Sifré to Numbers 1); and "Then the Israelites will say, 'If he who brought us out of Egypt and did the wonders and mighty deeds for us does not enter . . .'" (Sifré to Numbers 78).

While *Israel* therefore is the name of the social entity to which the Mishnah's authorship addresses its system, the fact remains that for the authorship of the Mishnah *Israel* does resonate as a differentiating category, with not-Israel, or *gentile*, the one routine antonym. Such a usage of *Israel* as a social entity very commonly occurs when someone wants for neutral purposes to distinguish Israelite from gentile: "If a majority is Israelite . . . , if a majority is gentile . . ." (M. Makh. 2:5, 7). *Israelite* in contradiction to *gentile* occurs in such ways as these: "A gentile who gave an Israelite . . . ," (M. Hal. 3:5); "He who sells to a gentile in the Land [of Israel] or to an Israelite outside of the Land [of Israel] . . ." (M. Sheb. 5:7); "He who receives a field from an Israelite, a gentile, or a Samaritan . . ." (M. Dem. 6:1); "He who sells his field to a gentile, and an Israelite went and bought it from him . . ." (M. Git. 4:9); "The ox of a gentile that gored the ox of an Israelite . . ." and vice versa (M. B.Q. 4:3); "An Israelite women [daughter] should not serve as midwife to a gentile . . ." (M. A.Z. 2:1); and so on throughout that tractate.

These usages treat the gentile as one classification, an otherwise undifferentiated one. The gentile under all circumstances simply is an outsider, one not subject to the laws of the Torah (e.g., in connection with land ownership and the application of seventh year taboos), and the Israelite is another classification in that same connection. Genealogical origin with an Israelite, not a gentile, mother occurs at M. Bik. 1:4, Qid. 4:7. M. Ned. 3:11 treats *gentile* as the antonym of *Israelite*: "He who by vow prohibits himself from deriving benefit from an Israelite . . ." may derive benefit from a gentile. Along these same lines, *Israelite* as antonym for *gentile* occurs at M. Git. 9:8, "What Israelites tell you . . ."; M. Makh. 2:5 (so too M. A.Z. 4:11), "A village in which Israelites and gentiles dwell . . . ," and the like. The distinctions made in these usages, however, are not narrowly political. In many instances, the antonymic difference yields cultic results: "A gentile who separated heave-offering for produce belonging to an Israelite . . ." (M. Ter. 1:1). If on the Sabbath a gentile performs an action for his or her own purposes, an Israelite may derive benefit from that action (M. Shab. 16:8; 23:4). In connection with the prohibition of leaven on Passover, what belongs to a gentile is not subject to the taboo (M. Pes. 2:3). *The uncircumcised* is taken to be a synonym for *gentile*, as *the circumcised* is for an Israelite male, so that if one takes a vow not to derive benefit from the uncircumcised the sense is understood not literally but figuratively; that is, circumcised gentiles are included in the vow, uncircumcised Israelites are excluded from it. Certain descriptive statements distinguish Israelite women from gentile women (M. Nid. 2:1).

Israel as People in Leviticus Rabbah

My claim that for the Judaism of the dual Torah, "Israel" viewed as nation or people forms a supernatural category comparable to the figure of Christ or the church finds ample documentation in Leviticus Rabbah. The relevance of that work's compilation about 400 to 450 C.E. should not be missed. Paul obviously cannot have allowed me to cite a book he did not read and cannot have read, but he would have admitted into evidence the reading of Scripture that a Judaic sage could have formulated—and did formulate in due course. Once Scripture forms the source of acknowledged facts for each party, the reading of Scripture in age succeeding age frames the legitimate issue for debate at any time.

In Leviticus Rabbah, as we have seen in a prior context, sages read the laws of Leviticus, which concern the ongoing sanctification of the life of Israel, as an account of the rules of the one-time salvation in history of the polity of Israel. To the framers of Leviticus Rabbah, one point of emphasis proved critical: Israel remains Israel, the Jewish people, after the flesh, not just because Israel today continues the family begun by Abraham, Isaac, Jacob, Joseph, and the other tribal founders and bears the heritage bequeathed by them. Israel is what it is also because of Israel's character as holy nation.

Salvific issues addressed not solely to individuals but to con-

cerns of history and eschatology frame themselves as political, dealing with corporate social entities. Maintaining, as the Christian
theologians did, that Israel would see no future salvation amounted
to declaring that Israel, the Jewish people (no longer merely a family), pursued no worthwhile purpose in continuing to endure. Indeed, in light of Paul's use of the metaphor of genealogy, the metaphor of the family could not serve to convey the proposition that
Israel (after the flesh) had had its salvation in the return to Zion and
would have no future salvation at all. Accordingly, from the perspective of the Christian theologian, the shift from genealogical to
political metaphors was necessary. When the argument joined the
question, Who is Israel? to the question, Who enjoys salvation? the
metaphor therefore shifted from family to political entity.

We find in Leviticus Rabbah clear address to the political metaphor, that is, the position that Israel constitutes a polity, not therefore conforming to a genealogical metaphor at all. I can find no
more suitable way of recapitulating the sages' reply to the linked
questions, Who is Israel? and, Is Israel saved? than by a brief survey
of one of the sustained essays they present on the subject in Leviticus
Rabbah. For that purpose we proceed briefly to survey the unfolding, in Leviticus Rabbah, Parashah 2, of the theme *Israel is precious*.
At Lev. R. II:III.2.B, we find an invocation of the genealogical justification for the election of Israel:

> **Leviticus Rabbah II:III**
>
> 2. B. He said to him, "Ephraim, head of the tribe, head of the
> session, one who is beautiful and exalted above all of my sons will
> be called by your name: [Samuel, the son of Elkanah, the son
> of Jeroham,] the son of Tohu, the son of Zuph, an Ephraimite"
> [1 Sam. 1:1]; "Jeroboam son of Nabat, an Ephraimite" [1 Kings
> 11:26]. "And David was an Ephraimite, of Bethlehem in Judah"
> (1 Sam. 17:12).

Because Ephraim, that is, Israel, had been exiled, the deeper message cannot escape our attention. Whatever happens, God loves
Ephraim. However Israel suffers, God's love endures, and God
cares. In context, this is framed as a genealogy. But in fact, the
matter in the syllogistic presentation of the passage at hand extends
not to family but to a social entity defined in other terms entirely.

That message brings powerful reassurance. Facing a Rome gone Christian, the sages had to state the obvious—which no longer seemed self-evident at all. What follows spells out this very point: God is especially concerned with Israel—again, viewed not as a family but as a social group of unrelated persons:

Leviticus Rabbah II:IV

2. A. "Speak to the children of Israel" (Lev. 1:2).

B. R. Yudan in the name of R. Samuel b. R. Nehemiah: "The matter may be compared to the case of a king who had an undergarment, concerning which he instructed his servant, saying to him, 'Fold it, shake it out, and be careful about it!'

C. "He said to him, 'My lord, O king, among all the undergarments that you have, [why] do you give me such instructions only about this one?'

D. "He said to him, 'It is because this is the one that I keep closest to my body.'

E. "So too did Moses say before the Holy One, blessed be He, Lord of the Universe: 'Among the seventy distinct nations that you have in your world, [why] do you give me instructions only concerning Israel? [For instance,] "Command the children of Israel" [Num. 28:2], "Say to the children of Israel" [Exod. 33:5], "Speak to the children of Israel'" [Lev. 1:2].

F. "He said to him, 'The reason is that they stick close to me, in line with the following verse of Scripture: "For as the undergarment cleaves to the loins of a man, so have I caused to cleave unto me the whole house of Israel"'" (Jer. 13:11).

Here the metaphor of family plays no role; the metaphor of Israel as corporate polity predominates. Note the phrase "They stick close to me." That is an appeal not to genealogy but to a different type of trait entirely. Israel is a social entity by reason of its relationship to God. Cleaving to God involves a way of life and a worldview that is distinctive and singular, and these are what mark Israel as singular. This passage applies a metaphor not of family but of people or nation, that is, a polity defined by external traits of belief and behavior, rather than inherent ones of genealogy. This quite distinct approach to the metaphor appropriate to Israel therefore is different from, though it complements, the one that speaks of Israel after the flesh.

G. Said R. Abin, "[The matter may be compared] to a king who had a purple cloak, concerning which he instructed his servant, saying, 'Fold it, shake it out, and be careful about it!'

H. "He said to him, 'My Lord, O king, among all the purple cloaks that you have, [why] do you give me such instructions only about this one?'

I. "He said to him, 'That is the one that I wore on my coronation day.'

J. "So too did Moses say before the Holy One, blessed be He, Lord of the Universe: 'Among the seventy distinct nations that you have in your world, [why] do you give instructions to me only concerning Israel? [For instance,] "Say to the children of Israel," "Command the children of Israel," "Speak to the children of Israel.'"

K. "He said to him, 'They are the ones who at the [Red] Sea declared me to be king, saying, "The Lord will be king'" (Exod. 15:18)."

The point of the passage has to do with Israel's particular relationship to God: Israel cleaves to God, declares God to be king, and accepts God's dominion. Further evidence of God's love for Israel derives from the commandments themselves. God watches over every little thing that Jews do, even caring what they eat for breakfast. That is what marks Israel off from other peoples, who form a common genus but diverse species. The emphasis on the keeping of the laws of the Torah as a mark of hope finds fulfillment here: the laws testify to God's deep concern for Israel. So there is sound reason for high hope, expressed in particular in keeping the laws of the Torah.

How does Israel win and retain God's favor? First, Israel knows how to serve God in the right way. Second, the nations, though they do what Israel does, do things wrong:

Leviticus Rabbah V:VIII
1. A. R. Simeon b. Yohai taught, "How masterful are the Israelites, for they know how to find favor with their creator. . . ."

E. Said R. Hunia [in Aramaic:], "There is a tenant farmer who knows how to borrow things, and there is a tenant farmer who does not know how to borrow. The one who knows how to borrow combs his hair, brushes off his clothes, puts on a good face, and then goes over to the overseer of his work to borrow from him. [The overseer] says to him, 'How's the land doing?' He says to him, 'May you have the merit of being fully satisfied with its [wonderful] produce.' 'How are the oxen doing?' He says to him, 'May you have the merit of being fully satisfied with their fat.' 'How are the goats doing?' 'May you have the merit of being fully satisfied with their young.' 'And what would you like?' Then he says, 'Now if you might have an extra ten denars, would you give them to me?' The overseer replies, 'If you want, take twenty.'

F. "But the one who does not know how to borrow leaves his hair a mess, his clothes filthy, his face gloomy. He too goes over to the overseer to borrow from him. The overseer says to him, 'How's the land doing?' He replies, 'I hope it will produce at least what [in seed] we put into it.' 'How are the oxen doing?' 'They're scrawny.' 'How are the goats doing?' 'They're scrawny too.' 'And what do you want?' 'Now if you might have an extra ten denars, would you give them to me?' The overseer replies, 'Go, pay me back what you already owe me!' "

As is clear, the traits that matter do not derive from ancestors but from the contemporary conduct of like-minded persons: a social group, not a family, and among social groups, a polity, or, in metaphorical language, a people or nation.

That brings us to the matter of opposites. Christ and anti-Christ find their counterparts in what I may call Israel and anti-Israel. Rome, in one setting the brother and heir to the same mother and father, in another is the nemesis: it is everything Israel is not, which tells us, also, what Israel is in this context.

The Opposite of Election: Rome as the Anti-Israel

This brings us to Rome as not only or mainly family, but Rome as a state—a nation, a people—within the genus of Israel as a nation or people. The reason is simple. In what is to follow, we see how Rome as family shades over into Rome as empire and state, comparable to Israel as a nation or state—and as the coming empire too. That shading explains why I have called the treatment of Rome a special problem. For while Rome stands for Esau, the metaphorization of Rome moves into fresh ground, comparing Rome to animals as well as to the near family. We have already seen the adumbration of the position that, in Leviticus Rabbah, would come to remarkably rich expression.

Rome stood for much more than merely a place among other places, or even a people or nation among other peoples or nations. Rome took up a place in the unfolding of the empires—Babylonia, Media, Greece, then Rome. Israel takes its place in that unfolding pattern, and hence is consubstantial with Babylonia, Media, Greece, and Rome. Thus, Rome and Israel form counterparts and opposites.

In this context, Rome functions in relationship to Israel as does the anti-Christ in relationship to Christ. Rome is next to last, Israel, last, in the sequence of empires. Rome is the penultimate empire on earth. Israel will constitute the ultimate one. That message, seeing the shifts in world history in a pattern and placing Israel at the apex of the shift, directly and precisely takes up the issue made urgent: the advent of the Christian emperors. Rome, among the successive empires, bears special traits, most of which derive from its distinctively Christian character. Rome is like Israel in a way in which no other state or nation is like Israel; consequently, in the odd metaphors of Rome as an animal unlike other animals or Rome as an empire unlike other empires, we have to appeal to a special relationship between Rome and Israel. Like the anti-Christ and Christ, Rome emerges as both like and not like Israel in ways that no other nation is ever represented as like Israel; likewise, Israel is like Rome in ways that Israel is not like any other people or nation.

The most suggestive disposition of Rome moved beyond the metaphor of the family. Esau is compared to a pig. The reason for the aptness of this analogy is simple. The pig exhibits public traits expected of a suitable beast, in that it shows a cloven hoof, such as the laws of acceptable beasts require. But the pig does not exhibit the inner traits of a suitable beast, in that it does not chew a cud. Accordingly, the pig confuses and deceives. The polemic against Esau/Rome is simple. Rome claims to be Israel in that it adheres to the Old Testament, that is, the written Torah of Sinai. Specifically, Rome is represented as only Christian Rome can have been represented: it superficially *looks* kosher, but it is unkosher. Pagan Rome cannot ever have looked kosher, but Christian Rome, with its appeal to continuity with ancient Israel, could and did, and moreover it claimed to be kosher. It bore some traits that validated this claim, but lacked others. It would be difficult to find a more direct confrontation between two parties to an argument. The issue is the same—Who is the true Israel?—the proof texts are the same, and the proof texts are read in precisely the same way. Only the conclusions differ!

The polemic represented in Genesis Rabbah and Leviticus Rabbah by the symbolization of Christian Rome makes the simple point, first, that Christians are no different from, and no better than, pagans; they are essentially the same. Christians' claim of forming part of Israel then requires no serious attention. Since Christians came to Jews with precisely that claim, the sages' response—they are another Babylonia—bears a powerful polemical charge. But that is not the whole story. Second, just as Israel had survived Babylonia, Media, and Greece, so would they endure to see the end of Rome (whether pagan, whether Christian). There is a third point as well. Rome really does differ from the earlier, pagan empires, and that polemic shifts the entire discourse, once we hear its symbolic vocabulary properly. The new Rome really did differ from the old. Christianity was not merely part of a succession of undifferentiated modes of paganism. The symbols assigned to Rome attributed worse, more dangerous traits than those assigned to the earlier empires. The pig pretends to be clean, just as the Christians give the signs of adherence to the God of Abraham, Isaac, and Jacob. That much the passage concedes. But the pig is not clean, exhibiting some, but not all, of the required indications, and Rome is not Israel, even though it shares Israel's Scripture.

That brings us to that mixture of metaphors in which genealogy explains relationships between polities. Let us begin with a simple example of how ubiquitous the shadow of Ishmael/Esau/Edom/Rome is. Wherever the sages reflect on future history in Genesis Rabbah, their minds turn to their own day. They found the hour difficult because Rome, now Christian, claimed that very birthright and blessing that they understood to be theirs alone. Christian Rome posed a threat without precedent. Another dominion claimed the rights and blessings that sustained Israel. Wherever in Scripture they turned, the sages found comfort in the iteration that the birthright, the blessing, the Torah, and the hope—all belonged to them and to none other.

As the several antagonists of Israel stand for Rome in particular, so the traits of Rome, as the sages perceived them, characterized the biblical heroes. There is natural enmity between Israel and Rome. Esau hated Israel even while he was still in the womb. Jacob, for his part, revealed from the womb those virtues that would characterize him later on, as eager to serve God as Esau was eager to worship idols. Rome is not really a valid Israel, any more than a pig, despite its public traits, is a valid animal.

In the apocalypticizing of the animals of Lev. 11:4–8/Deut. 14:7—the camel, rock badger, hare, and pig—the pig, standing for Rome, again emerges as different from the others and more threatening than the rest. Edom does not pretend to praise God but only blasphemes. It does not exalt the righteous but kills them. These symbols concede nothing to Christian monotheism and veneration of the Torah of Moses (in its written medium). Of greatest importance, note that while all the other beasts bring further ones in their wake, the pig does not: "It does not bring another kingdom after it." It will restore the crown to the one who will truly deserve it, Israel. Esau will be judged by Zion (Obad. 1:21).

How has this symbolization delivered an implicit message? It is in the treatment of Rome as distinct from but essentially equivalent to the former kingdoms. This seems to me a stunning way of saying that the now-Christian empire in no way requires differentiation from its pagan predecessors. Nothing has changed, except matters have gotten worse. Beyond Rome, standing in a straight line with the others, lies the true shift in history, the rule of Israel and the cessation of the dominion of the pagan nations. Rome in the fourth century became Christian. The sages responded by facing that fact quite squarely and saying, "Indeed, it is as you say, a kind of Israel, an heir of Abraham as your texts explicitly claim. But we remain the sole legitimate Israel, the bearer of the birthright—we and not you. So you are our brother: Esau, Ishmael, Edom."

The contrast between Israel and Esau produced the following anguished observation. Here, Rome is not yet Christian, so far as the clear reference is concerned. Esau/Rome ruled now, but Jacob/ Israel would follow in due course; this claim is made explicit. Esau remains Jacob's brother, and Esau rules before Jacob will. The application to contemporary affairs cannot be missed, both in the recognition of the true character of Esau—a brother!—and in the interpretation of the future. Representing Israel as singular invokes a narrowly political metaphor: nation or people, in the same genus as others, but, among them, singular and special by reason of service to God. But as soon as Rome enters the discourse, however, that original metaphor fails, for reasons I regard as intrinsic to the conflicting claims. Rome too claims to serve God, the same God in the same way. The political metaphor fails even while the political issues prevail, but at stake is God's portion in humanity.

Israel and God

Members of an ethnic group share a common religion, to be sure, but how they characterize their relationship with God certainly helps us to understand whether or not their ethnic ties bind God tightly to the group and close the group off from the rest of humanity. Conspicuous by its absence from the ethnic formulation is the issue of how God enters into matters. Yet, when we examine how holy Israel is portrayed in relationship to God, we find that same aspiration to form a worthy community in the service of the living God that Christians aim to realize in this world. For those Christians for whom Jesus Christ represents God's entry into this world, for example, the conception of Israel will prove intelligible, comparable to (though different from) their own idea of how God enters the world. Rabbinic Judaism invoked the conception of Israel to explain God's relationship to the world. Specifically, God left the world in stages because of Adam's actions and the actions of Adam's descendants, and God returned to the world in stages because of Abraham's actions and the actions of Abraham's descendants. So, as we noted at the outset of this chapter, Israel forms the medium by which God comes down to earth.

This conception is stated in the following terms: God entered the world on account of Israel, and God departed from the world because of Israel's actions. The center of God's presence was the Temple in its time, but the presence abandoned the Temple in due course.

When we speak of Jesus Christ, God incarnate, we invoke a category that is no more biographical or historical than Israel is ethnic. Israel evokes a variety of comparable categories in Christianity, at some points serving as the counterpart to the mystical body of Christ, the church; at other points as the counterpart to Jesus Christ, the opposite of Adam; and still elsewhere taking up other tasks in the theological enterprise. In this context, the treatment of rabbinic Judaism as ethnic and of Christianity as surpassing the ethnic proves incomprehensible.

The view of Israel's community as the locus, on earth, for God's presence comes to the surface in other ways as well. When Israel as a social entity is described, from a gathering of two persons on upward, the framers of Tractate Abot explicitly identify what they mean by a social entity: two or more persons where God is present, that is, where the Torah is studied. Here the Judaic counterpart to Christ is the Torah; but Israel serves in the familiar way of bringing God into the world, now through the medium of study of the Torah. We may then generalize as we did before. A social entity, a social group in particular—yet not called an Israel!—takes shape in one of two ways: either because people exchange Torah teachings, or because they do not do so. The one type of entity is differentiated from the other by that sole indicator, which conforms to the larger system at hand. Here we have another social entity that is sui generis, though it is not called (an) Israel.

Along these same lines, the individual and Israel serve as examples of the same thing, namely, God's love, which is all the greater because the person and the social entity are informed of that love.

Tractate Abot 3:14

A. He would say, "Precious is the human being, who was created in the image [of God]. It was an act of still greater love that it was made known to him that he was created in the image [of God]. As it is said, 'For in the image of God he made man' (Gen. 9:6)."

B. Precious is Israel (that is, are Israelites), who are called children to the Omnipresent. It was an act of still greater love that it was made known to them that they were called children to the Omnipresent, as it is said, "You are the children of the Lord your God" (Deut. 14:1).

C. Precious are Israelites, to whom was given the precious thing. It was an act of still greater love that it was made known to them that to them was given that precious thing with which the world was made, as it is said, "For I give you a good doctrine. Do not forsake my Torah" (Prov. 4:2).

Israel here means Israelite, not the social entity viewed as a collectivity, but those who belong to the entity—and therefore constitute that entity, even one by one. These are the children of the Lord, as Scripture says; Israelites are shown to be beloved because the Torah was given to them and because that fact was made known to them. In making these statements, the central issue is the Torah, not Israel. What is celebrated is the gift of the Torah.

The Family Nation, Sui Generis, in the Confrontation with Christianity

So we return, after a long passage through the writings of rabbinic Judaism, to our conversation with Paul. What have we to say in the end?

Just as Paul's doctrine of Israel responded to the issues addressed by his larger system, so the sages' doctrine of Israel formed in detail part of their systematic response to a larger systemic crisis. From the viewpoint of the Christians, the shift signified by the conversion of Constantine marked a caesura in history. The meaning of history commencing at the Creation pointed for Christians toward Christ's triumph in the person of the emperor and the institution of the Christian state. To Israel, the Jewish people as formed by the sages' system, what can these same events have meant? The received Scriptures of ancient and recent Israel—both Judaic and Christian—now awaited that same sort of sifting and selection that had followed earlier turnings of a notable order, in 586 B.C.E., and after 70 C.E., for example: which writing had now been proved right, which irrelevant? Christians asked this of themselves as they framed the canon of the Bible, both Old and New Testaments. Then Israel, the Jewish people, asked, what is the role and place for the received Torah of Sinai, in its diversity of scrolls?

The dogged faith that Jesus really was Christ, Messiah and king of the world, now found vindication in the events of the hour. What hope endured for the salvation of Israel in the future? In the hour of vindication the new Israel confronted the old, the one after the spirit calling into question the legitimacy of the one after the flesh: what now do you say of Christ? For Israel, the Jewish people, what was there to say in reply, not to Christ but to Christians? Three issues frame their, and our, principal concerns: the meaning of history, the realization of salvation, and the definition of one's own group in the encounter with the other.

To state matters simply, by claiming that Israel constituted Israel after the flesh, the actual, living, present family of Abraham and Sarah, Isaac and Rebecca, Jacob and Leah and Rachel, sages met head-on the Christian claim that there was—or could ever be—some other Israel and that the existing Jews no longer constituted that entity. By representing Israel as sui generis, the sages moreover focused on the systemic teleology, with its definition of salvation, in response to the Christian claim that salvation is not of Israel but of the church, now enthroned in this world as in heaven.

Christ's counterpart is Israel, Torah—and also the sage, just as Matthew represented him in the Sermon on the Mount. The sage, in the model of Moses, our rabbi, represented on earth the Torah that had come from heaven. The sage embodied what Israel was and was to be. So Israel as family in the model of the sage corresponded in its social definition to the church of Jesus Christ, the New Israel, the source of the salvation of humanity. The metaphors given prominence in the late fourth- and fifth-century sages' writings formed a remarkable counterpoint to the social metaphors important in the mind of significant Christian theologians, as both parties reflected on the political revolution that had taken place.

The social entity formed by the church or by Israel after the spirit or by the children of the promise, like the Israel of the Jews as they defined themselves, required a metaphor by which to account for itself. And revering the Scriptures, Christians too had long found in Israel the metaphor to account for its existence as a distinct social entity. The debate between Christians and Jews on Israel, and the broader problem of the social entity constituted by each, gained intensity because of a further peculiarity of the discourse between these two groups: both concurred that the group chosen by God would bear the name *Israel*. God's choice would settle the question. Jews, we know full well, saw themselves as the Israel joined in the flesh to the Israel of the scriptural record. Christians explained themselves as the Israel just formed among those saved by faith in God's salvation afforded by the resurrection of Jesus Christ. In these statements on who is Israel, the parties to the debate chose to affirm, each for its own part, its own unique legitimacy and to deny the other's right to endure at all as a social and national entity.

But both parties shared common premises as to definitions of issues and facts to settle the question.[2] They could mount a sustained argument between themselves because they talked about the same thing, invoked principles of logic in common, shared the definition of the pertinent facts. They differed only as to the outcome. The issue of who is Israel articulated in theological, not political, terms covers several topics: are the Jews today the Israel of ancient times? Was, and is, Jesus the Christ? If so, who are the Christians, both on their own and also in relationship to ancient Israel? These questions scarcely can be kept distinct from one another. All of them cover the familiar ground we have already traversed concerning the social entity, its teleology and (in concrete terms) salvation; that accounts for my insistence that we consider, in the context of defining Israel, a picture of salvation as the sages portrayed the matter.

The Christian agenda may be stated simply enough. First, was, and is, Jesus the Christ? If so, then the Jews who rejected him enjoyed no share in the salvation at hand. If not, then they do. The Christian challenge comes first. If Jesus was and is Christ, then Israel after the flesh, because of its unbelief, no longer enjoys the status of the people who bear salvation. Salvation has come, and Israel after the flesh has denied it. Jews and gentiles who have accepted him have received the promises of salvation and their fulfillment. The promises to Israel have been kept for them. There is a new Israel, one that is formed of the saved, as the prophets had said in ancient times that Israel would be saved.

Further issues that flowed from the first—the rejection of Jesus as Christ—concern the status of Israel, the Jewish people, now and in time to come. Israel after the flesh, represented from the Gospels forward as the people that rejected Jesus as Christ and participated in his crucifixion, claims to be the family of Abraham, Isaac, Jacob. First, does Israel today continue the Israel of ancient times? Israel maintains that Israel now continues in a physical and spiritual way the life of Israel then. Second, will the promises of the prophets to Israel afford salvation for Israel in time to come? Israel after the flesh awaits the fulfillment of the prophetic promise of salvation. The Christian position on these questions came to expression in a single negative: no, Israel today does not continue the Israel of old; no, the ancient promises will not again bear salvation, because they have already been kept; so, no, the Israel that declines to accept Jesus' claim to be the Christ is a nonpeople.

The response of Israel's sages to these same questions proves equally unequivocal. Yes, the Messiah will come in time to come, and yes, he will come to the Israel of today, which indeed continues the Israel of old. And yes, the Messiah will be a sage for the Israel in the model of sages. To state matters more abstractly, the Torah defined matters for the Israel of the sages as much as Christ defined matters for the Israel that had joined at the cross. So the issue is squarely and fairly joined. After this issue, the further question of who are the Christians requires close attention.

Before Christianity had addressed the issue of who the Christians were, Paul had already asked what the Jews were not. Christians formed the true people of God, so the old and lasting Israel, the Jewish people, did not. When Christians asked themselves what sort of group they formed, they formulated for themselves the problem of defining Israel that the sages worked out in their own way. In responding to this problem, Christians answered that they constituted a new group, and a group of a new type altogether. They identified with the succession to Israel after the flesh, with Israel after the spirit, with a group lacking all parallel or precedent, with God-fearers and law-keepers before Judaism was given at Sinai. The dilemma comes to expression in the statement of Eusebius, the biographer of Constantine and the founder of the Christian tradition of historiography in the fourth century:

> In the oracles directed to Abraham, Moses himself writes prophetically how in the times to come the descendants of Abraham, not only his Jewish seed but all the tribes and all the nations of the earth, will be deemed worthy of divine praise because of a common manner of worship like that of Abraham. . . . How could all the nations and tribes of the earth be blessed in Abraham if no relationship of either a spiritual or a physical nature existed be-

tween them? . . . How therefore could men reared amid an animal existence . . . be able to share in the blessings of the godly, unless they abandoned their savage ways and sought to participate in a life of piety like that of Abraham? . . .

Now Moses lived after Abraham, and he gave the Jewish race a certain corporate status which was based upon the laws provided by him. If the laws he established were the same as those by which godly men were guided before his time, if they were capable of being adopted by all peoples so that all the tribes and nations of the earth could worship God in accordance with the Mosaic enactments, one could say that the oracles had foretold that because of Mosaic laws men of every nation would worship God and live according to Judaism. . . . However, since the Mosaic enactments did not apply to other peoples but to the Jews alone . . . , a different way, a way distinct from the law of Moses, needed to be established, one by which the nations of all the earth might live as Abraham had so that they could receive an equal share of blessing with him.[3]

Because, with the advent of Constantine, a political dimension served to take the measure of the Christian polity, we have to ask about the political consciousness of the church in its original formulation. In this matter Adolph Harnack points out that the political consciousness of the church rests on three premises: first, the political element in the Jewish apocalyptic; second, the movement of the gospel to the Greeks; and third, the ruin of Jerusalem and the end of the Jewish state. He says, "The first of these elements stood in antithesis to the others, so that in this way the political consciousness of the church came to be defined in opposite directions and had to work itself out of initial contradictions."[4] From early times, Harnack says, the Christians saw Christianity as "the central point of humanity in the field of political history as well as its determining factor." That had been the Jews' view of themselves. With Constantine, the corresponding Christian conception matched reality.

One problem from the Christian theologians' perspective demanded a solution: the existing Israel, which revered the same Scriptures and claimed descent from ancient Israel. So long as the two parties to the debate shared the same subordinated political circumstance, Jewry could quite nicely hold its own in the debate. But with the shift in the politics of the empire, the terms of the debate changed. The Christian party to the debate began to invoke its familiar position with the power of the state.

The confrontation with Christianity, in the sages' thought, took the form of a family dispute about who was the legitimate heir to the same ancestor. The Judaic sages and Christian theologians addressed the issue in pretty much the same terms, with a single mode of argument, appealing to a shared body of facts—the Scriptures. Before we address the sages' position, let us rapidly survey the opposition's framing of the issue. To show us how a fourth-century Christian theologian addressed the question at hand, namely, who is Israel in the light of the salvation of Jesus Christ, we turn to Aphrahat, a Christian monk in Mesopotamia (ca. 300–350 C.E.), who wrote a sustained treatise on the relationship of Christianity and Judaism. Aphrahat deserves an extended hearing, because, like our sages, he framed matters solely by appeal to the shared facts of Scripture. He has the additional merit of presenting his arguments in a reasoned and objective manner, proposing to argue with equals about matters of shared concern and on the basis of a common premise.

Aphrahat's demonstrations, written in 337–344 C.E., take up issues facing the church in the Iranian Empire. He rarely cites the New Testament in his demonstrations on Judaism. Moreover, when he cites the Hebrew Scriptures, he ordinarily refrains from a fanciful or allegoristic reading of them, but, like the rabbis whose comments we have surveyed, he stressed that his interpretation rested solely on the obvious, factual meaning at hand. In that way he rejected the exegesis of the sages, with its power to read one thing in terms of something else. His arguments thus invoked rational considerations and historical facts: this is what happened, this is what it means. The Scriptures therefore present facts on which all parties concur— the basis for a family argument.

Let me point to Aphrahat's Demonstration 16, "On the Peoples Which Are in the Place of the People." Aphrahat's message is this: "The people Israel was rejected, and the peoples took their place. Israel repeatedly was warned by the prophets, but to no avail, so God abandoned them and replaced them with the gentiles. Scripture frequently referred to the gentiles as Israel. The vocation of the peoples was prior to that of the people of Israel, and from of old, whoever from among the people was pleasing to God was more justified than Israel: Jethro, the Gibeonites, Rahab, Ebedmelech the Ethiopian, Uriah the Hittite. By means of the gentiles God provoked Israel." First, Aphrahat maintains that "the peoples which were of all languages were called first, before Israel, to the inheritance of the Most High, as God said to Abraham, 'I have made you the father of a multitude of peoples' (Gen. 17:5). Moses proclaimed, saying, 'The peoples will call to the mountain, and there will they offer sacrifices of righteousness' (Deut. 33:19)." Not only so, but God further rejected Israel. That is why God turned to the peoples: "When he saw that they would not listen to him, he turned to the peoples, saying to them, 'Hear O peoples, and know, O church which is among them, and hearken, O land, in its fullness' (Jer. 6:18–19)." So who is now Israel? It is the peoples, no longer the old Israel: "By the name of Jacob [now] are called the people which is of the peoples."

This is the key to Aphrahat's case. The people that was a non-people, the people that had assembled out of the people, has now replaced Israel. Like Eusebius, Aphrahat maintained that the peoples had been called to God before the people of Israel. The people that was a nonpeople should not regard itself as alien to God: "If they should say, 'Us has he called alien children,' they have not been called alien children, but sons and heirs. . . . But the peoples are those who hearken to God and were lamed and kept back from the ways of their sins." Indeed, the peoples produced believers who were superior in every respect to Israel. Aphrahat here refers to the Gibeonites, Rahab, and various other gentiles mentioned in the scriptural narrative. So he concludes, "This brief memorial I have written to you concerning the peoples, because the Jews take pride and say, 'We are the people of God and the children of Abraham.' But we shall listen to John [the Baptist] who, when they took pride [saying], 'We are the children of Abraham,' then said to them, 'You should not boast and say, Abraham is father unto us, for from these very rocks can God raise up children for Abraham'" (Matthew 3:9).

In Demonstration 19, "Against the Jews, on Account of Their Saying That They Are Destined to Be Gathered Together," Aphrahat proceeds to the corollary argument, that the Israel after the flesh has lost its reason to endure as a nation. Why? Because no salvation awaits it in the future. The prophetic promises of salvation have all come to fulfillment in the past, and the climactic salvation for Israel, through the act of Jesus Christ, brought the salvific drama to its conclusion.

Aphrahat's argument can be summarized as follows: the Jews expect to be gathered together by the Messiah, but this expectation is in vain. God was never reconciled to them but has rejected them. The prophetic promises of restoration were all fulfilled in the return from Babylonia. Daniel's prayer was answered, and his vision was realized in the time of Jesus and in the destruction of Jerusalem. It will never be rebuilt. When, in 362–363 C.E., the emperor Julian (intending to embarrass Christianity) allowed Jews to undertake the rebuilding of the Temple in Jerusalem, the project failed. The outcome struck Christian theologians as decisive evidence of who is Israel, God's people, and who is not.

To Aphrahat's indictment of unbelieving Israel, the metaphor of family proves inconsequential. The political metaphor involving a people or nation takes over. For the challenge of those who held such views as Aphrahat expresses, the case is complete: the people that is a nonpeople, the people that is of the peoples, has taken the place of the people that claims to carry forward the salvific history of ancient Israel. The reason is twofold. First, Israel (not called "Israel after the flesh") has rejected salvation and so lost its reason to exist; and second, the nonpeople have accepted salvation and so gained its reason to exist.

The two issues as framed by the Christian theologians complement one another. Once the new people formed out of the peoples enters the status of Israel, then the old Israel loses that status. And how to express that judgment? By denying the premise of the life of Israel after the flesh, that salvation for the people of God would come in future time. If enduring Israel would never enjoy salvation, then it had no reason to exist: that is the premise of the argument framed in behalf of the people that had found its reason to exist (from its perspective) solely in its salvation by Jesus Christ. So what explained to the Christian community how that community had come into being also accounted for the anticipated disappearance of the nation that had rejected that very same nation-creating event.

Paul's solution, distinguishing children of the promise from children of the flesh, formed only one answer to the question, Who are you? Another answer invoked the notion that the Christians formed a new people, a third race. When the change came, with the Christianization of the Roman Empire at the highest levels of government, the new people, the third race, had to frame a position and policy about the old people, Israel after the flesh. The Christians from the beginning saw themselves as a people without a past, a nonpeople, a people gathered from the peoples. Then, who they can claim to be hardly derives from who they have been. Identifying with ancient Israel was a perfectly natural and correct initiative, well founded on the basis of the Christian canon, encompassing the Hebrew Scriptures as "the old testament." It admirably accounted for the Christian presence in humanity, provided a past, explained to diverse people what they had in common. If this Christianity transcended ethnic limits, so did the sages' Judaism—and in exactly the same ways, and for precisely the same reasons. Both spoke of things unseen, intangible, surpassing human understanding: that love of God that comes by grace, whether through Christ, whether through Israel. But, for our sages of blessed memory, it was solely through Israel, in that supernatural sense that everywhere defined how God came to dwell on earth, within humanity.

Now we must ask ourselves, why should we who witness the transition from the century of total war to an age we cannot now imagine care about this long-ago debate about who is Israel and what Scripture says? What is at stake in this matter of the ethnicity of an old religion? Why should anybody care who and what is Israel?

5

Religion, Nationality, and Ethnicity

WHAT IS AT STAKE in this debate about the character of Israel? It is the future of the Torah, which is to say, the knowledge of God in God's own self-manifestation. Will humanity know God through the Torah, or will humanity be denied the knowledge of God that the Torah conveys?[1] If the Jews form a merely ethnic group—or an ethnic group at all—then Judaism (that is, the Torah) is lost to them and to everybody else. How the Jews define themselves therefore bears heavy consequences for the future of humanity—or so the Torah insists.

In the United States today, Judaism is indistinguishable from the political opinions of Jews. No more ethnic definition of religion can emerge than the one that identifies with the Torah at Sinai those particular political positions that people happen to advocate at this particular moment. In this country and in Western Europe, the Jews form an ethnic group, which happens to call its places of ethnic assembly *synagogues* (the counterpart to churches) and in a desultory way conducts prayer as a preliminary to intense association, family gathering, intimate conversation, and the like. Judaism has been hijacked.

To understand what I mean, try to imagine an organization that adopts the following resolutions, and ask yourself, What kind of an organization is this? The organization resolves to actively oppose state and local referenda and statutes restricting the civil rights of gay men and lesbians. . . . The organization resolves to support the use of fetal tissue for the purpose of life-saving or life-enhancing research. . . . The organization resolves to advocate a single-payer system as the most likely means of fulfilling the principles articulated in past organization resolutions on health care reform. . . . The organization resolves to call on our federal, provincial, state, and local governments to adopt legislation that will afford partners in committed lesbian and gay relationships the means of legally acknowledging such relationships. . . . The organization resolves to support passage of legislation such as the omnibus Women's Health Equity Act. . . . And so on.

Reading these and similar resolutions, you would probably suppose that you had stumbled across a report of the National Organization of Women, or, more likely, the Reform Democratic Club of the Upper West Side of Manhattan. You might not suppose that you had just read a document from the Union of American Hebrew Congregations (UAHC) biennial meeting in 1993, a meeting run by the national organization of Reform Judaism in the United States. But that is precisely what you have read. Substitute *UAHC* for *organization* and you have the report on biennial resolutions in *Reform Judaism,* spring 1994 issue. The other resolutions—a call for religious pluralism in the state of Israel, support for the Israel-PLO declaration of principles, an appeal to commute Jonathan Pollard's sentence to time served, support for synagogues, and the like—represent more or less mainstream positions that are particular to Jewish organizations. Reading them, you would not mistake your location.

When the Jewish community gets together in its national organizations, the more one floats toward the mainstream, the less distinctively Jewish, and the more utterly un-Judaic, the agenda. Take, for example, the National Jewish Community Relations Advisory Council (NJCRAC). It is made up of representatives of most of the Jewish Community Federations throughout the United States, as well as of the American Jewish Committee, American Jewish Congress, B'nai B'rith/Anti-Defamation League, Hadassah, Jewish Labor Committee, Jewish War Veterans, National Council of Jewish Women, Union of American Hebrew Congregations, Union of Orthodox Jewish Congregations of America, United Synagogue of Conservative Judaism, Women's American Ort—pretty much everybody within the wall-to-wall organizational framework of U.S. Jewry. So what do they talk about?

Concerns for "community relations" include these topics: equal opportunity and social justice; Israel and the Middle East; world Jewry and international human rights; and Jewish security and the Bill of Rights. Of these topics, concern for anti-Semitism, Jews in the former Soviet Union, the Holocaust, and the like belongs well within the framework of distinctively Jewish engagements. But what can we make of topics such as these: poverty and the urban agenda; children at risk; immigration and refugee policy; public school education; health care issues; status of women. If you have to be Jewish to care about Jews in the Soviet Union, you certainly don't have to be Jewish to talk about public school education.

Why does the Jewish community adopt as its particularly, distinctively Jewish issue the support of public education to the exclusion of private education? Only the Union of Orthodox Jewish Congregations of America dissented, insisting that the Jewish community support "properly drawn educational choice programs that can constitutionally and equitably provide funds for non-public school students." Only that group stated, "We regret the wooden application of the establishment clause reflected in the NJCRAC position."

What makes an umbrella organization of the Jewish community want to "urge the Administration and Congress to consider as a top priority developing policies and strategies that focus on blighted urban areas, including rebuilding urban infrastructure . . . educate the public about the scope and causes of poverty and the need for more vigorous public policies to deal with poverty . . ."? Why does it take the Jewish community in particular to "urge expansion of job training, apprenticeship, and community service programs that equip teenagers with job skills that will enable them to find meaningful employment"? And on and on.

In other words, what we have here is not the organized Jewish community addressing its particular and legitimate concerns, but the circumcised sector of the Democratic Party, reviewing the party's current policy and endorsing it. Just as the Communists in the bad old days organized *Yevsektzia*—the Jewish Bureau—which through Jewish agitators manipulated Jewish opinion for the party's purposes, so the organized Jewish community serves as the Jewish Bureau of the liberal establishment. Its issues, its emphases, its con-

cerns predominate—and the concerns of centrist America, our issues, our emphases, our concerns never register. It goes without
saying that the bulk of the Reform, Reconstructionist, and Conservative rabbinate, and a fair number of Orthodox rabbis as well, do
yeoman service as cheerleaders for left-wing zealotry.

I see three problems here. First, Judaism clearly plays no role in
the organized Jewish community. Like the separation of church and
state, the organized Jewish community maintains the rigid and absolute separation of Judaism from Jewry. Examining the NJCRAC
program, with its utterly secular concerns, leaves no doubt on that
score. Second, when a Judaic religious organization meets, as in the
case of the Reform movement, whatever currently defines the style
of the left becomes God's will, so that a religion that proclaims "to
life" takes a stand for abortion and against the life of the fetus, in
direct contradiction to the Torah; that treats marriage as ordained
by God from Adam and Eve onward wants two Adams and no Eve
in its Eden; and that teaches us about God finds it possible to adopt
a dozen resolutions but not once speak of the Torah of Sinai. Third,
Judaism finds itself harnessed to the service of this morning's fash-
ions among limousine liberals. From the perspective of the Torah,
what is principal has been made subordinate.

To broaden the frame of reference, we perceive the crisis of self-
definition—Is Israel a religious or ethnic group?—as acute, not
merely chronic, when we turn to the European counterpart. There,
uniting religion and ethnicity, language, territory, and nationality is
as European as ethnic cleansing and the Holocaust. Religion, nationality, and ethnicity join in Europe to state in a single voice to the
rest of the world, "We are God's—and you can go to hell." In the
worst cases, "we" then will gladly help "you" on your way. In most
cases, "we" simply keep our distance from an alien, undifferentiated
outside.

Religion forms a principal medium for the disruption of societies
that bear the burden of real differences, as most European nations
do, or for the alienation of nations that, unified in ethnic and linguistic and religious commonality, turn their backs on everybody
else—which covers the rest of Europe. Whether in polyglot, religiously diverse Yugoslavia and Germany or in linguistically, culturally, and ethnically uniform Finland and Poland and Sweden, reli-

gion preaches humanity in God's image but practices the brutal, vulgar discrimination between us and them, which leaves those who are different feeling like outsiders (as in Finland and Sweden) or subject to unashamed brutality (as in Poland and Russia and Germany).

Peoples in the European mosaic do not account for themselves solely by an appeal to a unique language and genealogy; nor do they explain themselves through a defining history and deeply particular, expressive literature; nor do they invoke the innate taste that they but not others feel in their blood and bones, preferences for the local specialties of clumsy, boring music, cuisine flavored in a special way (the bland and utterly tasteless Karelian puddings of Finland come to mind) and odd, childish costumes, put on for strange occasions (such as the leather shorts worn in Bavaria worn to honor the first beer of the new season). No, these alone do not explain the racism of the European ethnic nationalities.

These peoples, all aspiring to the status of empowered, political nations, also add to the mixture a powerful catalyst "God loves us, in particular." Without a religion, the particularities of language, territory, innate memory, and other racist categories may well do their disruptive work, but we have few instances where they do. Common sense excludes the mere trivialities of a distinctive myth or secular difference. In most instances of protracted conflict among distinct national-ethnic groups, religion makes the rest cohere—and vastly raises what is at stake. If I deliberately, wantonly kill you, it is murder. If in the name of God I kill you, it is an act not of patriotism alone, but of piety.

The consequence can be predicted. Contempt for the other, created out of religious attitudes, forms the underside of ethnicity infused with religious particularity. Everyone feels it—especially the victims of everybody else's exclusionary ethnicity. When the chief rabbi of Hungary told other Hungarians that, without the Jews, all Hungary could claim as its own was the local apricot wine and embroidered peasant blouses, he embarrassed himself and outraged his fellow citizens. But he also expressed a quite familiar attitude throughout Europe: without us, you do not count; with us, we alone count. It is difficult to identify an *us* without its particular God at the heart of matters.

The fault lines of Europe's plate tectonics run down religious fissures: Orthodox versus Roman Catholic versus Islam accounts for the breakdown of social order in the former Yugoslavia's Serbia, Croatia, and Bosnia, as everybody knows; Ukraine breaks into Roman Catholic and not so; Poland is Poland by reason of the Virgin—and by reason of anti-Semitism, even after all the Jews have left or been murdered; the English, secular to themselves, are Protestant to the Irish Catholics; Belgium breaks into Catholic and Protestant; and so on. Anyone who calls into doubt the power of religion to create bigots need only examine in its fullness the virulently racist anti-Semitism of the newly liberated Russian Orthodox Church. We do not have to venture to India or East Timor or Indonesia to find how ethnicity and religiosity unite and, in their fusion, burst the bonds of social order.

Any case against the proposition that Judaism, too, is essentially an ethnic celebration has to weigh in the balance the case for that proposition. The truth is that the ethnic vastly outweighs the religious in the practiced Judaism of Europe and the United States.[2] And if the given of Paul's distinction between the ethnic and the religious in Judaism derives from the larger logic of his systemic problem—how to accommodate gentiles within the Torah yet outside the legal requirements thereof—the case for the ethnicity of Judaism does not require Paul's testimony. In our own time, as in times past, ethnicity has taken priority over religiosity in the definition of who and what Israel is.

But that other Judaism, the Judaism of our sages of blessed memory, also flourishes, and the faithful to that Judaism do form its Israel. They validate my insistence on the supernatural Israel as the native category of Judaism. These Jews, this Israel appears the most segregated. Yet, when we hear their prayers and their singing studies, we recognize the music: the Te Deum sung in Torah study. Different in everything but the things that count, the segregated Jews show that Paul was right about the surface of things, but wrong about the heart and soul: Judaism is not about Israel but about God's search for humanity, and the Torah is God's way of purifying the heart of those made "in our image, after our likeness." At stake then is not ethnic but exemplary Israel, a very different thing.

Given the teachings we have examined, we must find puzzling the profoundly ethnic character of much of contemporary diaspora Judaism. The Israel of our sages of blessed memory is real, but not tangible; it appeals to a genealogy that comes not in bones or blood but in a commonality of spirit formed in the Torah. This Israel knows nothing of the frontiers of language or race or condition or gender. This Judaic (not merely Jewish) Israel finds its definition not in the closed borders of this world but in the passage opened by God to humanity through the Torah of Sinai, offered to all peoples, accepted by only one people.

Nothing in the authoritative sources of Judaism we have examined therefore prepares us for a Judaism that speaks the language of this-worldly and merely tangible uniqueness, palpable family and ethnic genealogy, nation and people, but does not mean to invoke God's presence in humanity. An exclusionary Judaism stands against every line we have examined in the preceding chapters. But it characterizes most of those who, calling themselves Jews, also profess a religion they deem Judaism and they define out of the very books we have considered here.

It is not so hard to understand, however, when we recall the human situation to which Judaism—as distinct from the Torah of our sages of blessed memory—addresses itself. Few in number, Jews compensate by other measures. To understand the current state of Judaism, we take Uppsala, for example, and its Jewish community, numbering perhaps a hundred in a city of tens of thousands. In Uppsala, contrast Judaism to Christianity: the one weak, impoverished, few, and old; the other, dominant, powerful, world-embracing. There, in the heartland and birthplace of Sweden, the particular place where Christian Sweden locates itself, on one hill overlooking a great vista stands a castle, on the same high ridge, the cathedral. Here the kings and queens of Sweden are crowned; here they are buried, in a massive, proud, enduring construction of a thousand years. Or come to Åbo (Turku) in Finland, with its cathedral, seat of the Church of Finland, and burial place of heroes of the country. Or to Westminster, in London, and so from capital to capital; not necessarily where the government of the moment sits, but where the heart of the nation beats.

We walk across Uppsala and make our way down the hill where

the cathedral and the university look down on the plain. There, across town, in a working-class apartment house, in a room provided by the municipality when it has the funds, a tiny Jewish community, made up of survivors of the Holocaust, a few Swedish-born Jewish students at the university, and whoever happens by, comes together now and then. In a room furnished with junk—planks for tables, a floor unswept—on the shelves of the Jewish community synagogue in Uppsala are a few score of books from the 1930s (when someone got around to buying a couple of books about British land policy in Palestine) and some tattered Pentateuchs and prayerbooks. In contrast, the elegantly decorated cathedral stands a hundred yards from one of the world's great libraries.

Contrast—as Buber did before the mighty Lutheran and Catholic cathedrals of Worms, Germany—the pride of Christianity with the humble circumstances of Judaism here, and you understand the challenge to Israel in Europe—or in other parts of the world, including the Near East—and its response. The late master of Judaic learning, Harry A. Wolfson, told me of the vision that infused his life. As a young man coming to Harvard, he found his way into the stacks of the great Widener Library, where, side by side, he found the holy books of Christianity and Judaism. The one set of books stood upright, elegantly printed, richly bound in leather, all in place. The other lay strewn about, the bindings broken, the paper yellowing. He determined that, in his life, he would restore the books of Judaism to their rightful place on the shelves: in proper bindings, in right array, and in order.

Dwelling side by side with mighty Islam and ancient Christianity, each with vast territories and monuments to God in the here and now, what has Israel to show for itself? Who can blame the fleas for telling the dog how much they matter? If Christianities transform a universal religion into ethnic religiosities, so do Judaisms. It does not improve matters for Judaism to say, well, there are reasons. There always are reasons. But the facts give testimony nonetheless.

How would our sages have stood in judgment upon their professed heirs and successors? They set forth their Israel as sui generis. Their heirs invoke the language of uniqueness to speak not of the faith, the Torah, but of the group called into being by the faith. What is unique about the Israel of our sages is the holy way of life through which God sanctified the ordinary ways of a common people. What is unique about the Jewish people today, so it is broadly insisted on, is the Holocaust. But as principal voices of Holocaust theology have insisted, our blood is no redder than that of any other victims. Our claim to a unique place in the hierarchy of victims is not, I think, what our sages had in mind as setting holy Israel apart from the nations of the world.

Why do these things matter, whether to holy Israel or to the rest of humanity? At stake in the past is always, and only, the formation of the future. Even though most of this book is taken up with the presentation and exposition of how the Judaism of the sages treats the theme of Israel, I think that the issue of the ethnicity of Judaism's Israel is urgent. The facts come from a distant past of ancient writings, but they relate to the world to which I address the evidence at hand. I conceive this evidence to form a model and an alternative, one that demands a hearing, that insists on a presence in the religious world of contemporary humanity.

The issue of ethnicity in religion takes shape in the headlines of one region today and in another region tomorrow, and the century that now dawns, like many over times past, will mark an age of ethnic conflict formulated in religious terms. It is fitting that a religion long described as merely ethnic by its enemies, and today perceived as national and as ethnic by its own faithful, should step forward and speak for itself. As I have shown, that religion, the Judaism of the dual Torah, no less than Christianity as founded by Jesus and formulated by Paul, solved the ethnic problem and formulated a theory of the social order that transcended the merely ethnic and addressed the whole of humanity in the name of the one God and creator of all humanity.

Our own century marked the breakdown of long-established rules of orderly coexistence among diverse religious groups sharing the same land. Polyglot, multiethnic, religiously diverse empires gave way to nation-states, each with its locus in its church. The union of religious, ethnic, national, political, and even economic structures brought about convulsions disastrous for the social order, with world wars as the consequence. Europe suffered the breakdown; America, at the head of the rest of the world, was left to try to pick up the pieces.

We Americans have learned something out of our society, which I think is congruent to the universal Christianity set forth by Jesus and Paul and the universal Judaism set forth by our sages of blessed memory. Jesus called the humble and poor and weak, whether of Israel or Samaria. Paul spoke to Jew and gentile. Our sages of blessed memory received as fully Israel anyone who came under the wings of God's presence and accepted the Torah of Sinai. So Christianity and Judaism differentiated among humanity by distinctions not of blood and language and race and nationality, but of conviction and conscience and condition.

I said earlier that I thought we Americans have something to teach that in its way forms a deeply Christian and Judaic formulation of the matter of ethnicity: social difference in the here and now of tangible things. Let me say why. To us Americans, ours is a less imposing, and therefore more perfect, union. We define Americanness without invoking the categories of religion or ethnicity, and we also do not take for granted that to belong to a given ethnic group is also to subscribe to its official religion. Americans see matters differently, and that is why I think Europeans have important lessons to learn from us. We recognize difference, but we find reasons for living together in full recognition of that difference.

Just as Jesus spoke of God's love, which transcends ethnic limits, and just as Paul appealed to Greek and Jew alike, and just as our sages of blessed memory defined their Israel in supernatural terms, so we Americans in our secular language deliver the same message. True, we fail to heed our own message. We may legitimately take pride only in what we have to say, but not in what we then go out and do. Granted, our message pertains to this-worldly nationality, the Judaic and the Christian messages to matters of God's perspective on humanity. But the stakes are much the same: we must define our *us* so as to leave ample space for the *other*.

Where did I first ask myself questions about religion, nationality, and ethnicity, and so begin four decades of reflection that come to a conclusion in these pages? I discovered America in German Europe, Judaism in Christian America.

It was in Europe as a very young man that I learned the difference between American and European nationality. As a student at Oxford forty years ago, fleeing the gloom of the English winter for the sun of Italy, I came home via Germany. A German friend from Harvard days—he used to help me with my German language class—had invited me to visit him in Frankfurt. When I came to Oxford, in September 1953, Gerald Reitlinger's *The Final Solution* was on the shelves at a local bookstore. Since, then as now, I read pretty much whatever came to hand, and certainly anything about the Jews, I bought it and read it. Within a day, I wrote to my friend in Germany and accepted his invitation; who can have been the people who did these things, of which, before reading *The Final Solution,* I had been only dimly aware?

I took the train from Italy, and my friend met me at the railroad station with his father. Bearing an invented, purely American name, with no European antecedents known to my father's mother, the only link to the lost past, it never occurred to me that I would be thought of German origin. The name meant nothing, so far as I knew. But Neusner is close enough to a good German name, Neuser, to be deemed *echt-Deutsch.* And to Germans, a German was (and, alas, is) either a Protestant or a Catholic, not a Jew, not a Muslim. So what kind was I?

The first thing my friend's father asked me, as we left the station, was, "Herr Neusner, sind sie Katholisch oder Evangelisch?" ("Mr. Neusner, are you Catholic or Protestant?") He took for granted I stemmed from German roots, so the question was natural, Germans being one or the other. He also assumed his son would not invite a German of Jewish parentage to his home.

Responding to a strange look from my friend, I reckoned "None of the above" was not the right answer, and, since I was pretty sure I could not be a Catholic by any standard. I said, "Etwas Evanglisch," by which I hoped I was saying, "Well, some strange species of protestant," with a very small *p.* He seemed satisfied and turned my attention to the ruins of Germany, for, in December 1953, much of downtown Frankfurt had been reduced to rubble.

My friend later explained to me, "As a presumed gentile, you will see more and hear more than as a Jew; if they know you're a Jew, everybody will be nervous and nice—and very, very circumspect." He was right—I saw the generation of Germans who, if they didn't perpetrate the Holocaust, then at least thought Hitler was right in everything he did but that, and thought we Americans committed a historical error in fighting against Hitler rather than Stalin. I met the winner of a Hitler prize for a novel; a judge of the "old days"; executives of I. G. Farben, a manufacturer of motor-cycles, which, during the war, had made "other things"—middle-rank Nazis one and all; and, of course, every one of them had hidden a Jew in his basement through the war, so each one had told me with a perfectly straight face. I was not there to ask too many questions. I took it all in.

I didn't have to ask any to learn what I had come to find out: who are the people who did these things? Later on, as my un-German eating habits emerged—even as a Reform Jew in those days, I didn't eat ham or pork—the parents drew the right conclusion, and became very quiet. The conclusion I drew was that Germans could not imagine a German who was not Christian, either Protestant or Catholic (no Orthodox Christians need apply). To be German was to be both German by birth to a German by birth, backward to the Teutonic tribes, and to be a Western Christian. The union of the ethnic (birth, genealogy), the linguistic (German, with our accent), the cultural (our taste in local wine and beer), and above all, the territorial formed the absolute given in the father's construction of the world. That is when and where I discovered American exceptionalism and went in search of its Judaic (and therefore also its Christian) counterpart.

It was in the model of America that I began to think about the power of Judaism and Christianity to define *us* without having to exclude everybody else. In the Protestant West Hartford of those days, we celebrated the Pilgrim Fathers as ours too, we Americans who were also Italian or Polish Catholics or Reform or Conservative Jews. So Guy Pastor, Clair Kramarszyk, and Jack Neusner—not only Alden Leavenworth and Betsy Steadman—sang, "We gather together to ask the Lord's blessing." The Pilgrim Fathers were ours too. No one explained how; everyone took it for granted (or so we imagined).

Americans all, that's what the teachers said, Miss Melcher, Miss Ring, Miss Staples, Mr. Roberts, and my favorite of all time, Miss Ardis B. Chase, a Yankee from down east in Maine, who told me to learn how to write and then taught me what she meant. And she said to me, every day I think, "Jack, *illegitimae non carborundum,*" which was Yankee for, "Don't let the bastards wear you down." I never did: I was never "you people" to Miss Chase. Being her student, writing coherent sentences—to her that was my nationality, coming to me from a Yankee from down east who knew the meaning of the word *tough* and why it belonged with the word *American*. (And, I added, with the word *Jewish*, too.)

The world has not changed. We Americans continue to define Americanness—belonging to the national community by right, not by sufferance—in our own way. To us it is the place we live, but not where we come from; the language we speak—our own American English—and not the language our immigrant ancestors spoke; the shared affirmations of a national consensus, not the received and special revelation some acknowledge and others ignore. How this view of *we* as against *the rest* comes to expression varies, but two and a quarter centuries after our nation gained its independence, it is clear that we define difference and sameness in categories other than those that govern in Europe and the rest of the world. That explains, also, why the Judaic and Christian religions in this country have formed a different relationship from the one that prevails across Europe. Christians labor at forming a respectful vision of Judaism, and Judaists—the faithful of Judaism—struggle appropriately to respond, and do respond in the same spirit.

We are Americans by nationality, all of us, and that nationality finds its definition in more, much more, than the color of our passports. It defines our way of living together; it comes to realization in the bases for social order that hold us in one coherent structure and system. Our nationality appeals not to race or blood, which by definition one has or does not have, but to conviction and character and conscience, which by definition all of us may freely attain. We have defined nationality so as to accommodate anyone from anywhere in the world. Everyone knows that is how Christianity defines religion, and, in these pages, I have shown that is also how Judaism defines religion.

American nationality finds its definition not in race or religion, but in language and territory and region and locality, and also in a set of iron convictions that come to expression in the Constitution, the Bill of Rights, and the institutions of democratic government that now form the oldest continuing secular-political structure on the face of the earth. For us Americans, therefore, the union of religion and ethnicity presents a formidable puzzle. Ethnicity joined to religion and extended to nationality for us eludes comprehension. The reason is not only that we have no state church, though the First Amendment, defining religion as a native category but also denying religions political preferment, forms a considerable source of our capacious nationality. It is also that we do not possess the experience of a social world formed by lands divided in such a way. Our country holds us all, has room for us all. And the religions of America have responded with a corresponding vision of religion: a Judaism that seeks the Israel formed by our sages of blessed memory, a Christianity that looks to the model of Jesus and the doctrine of Paul for the foundation of a holy Israel.

What is at theological stake? In the Judaism set forth in the normative writings, the outsider who accepts the Torah as given by God becomes fully Israel. His or her offspring then take their place in Israel, without differentiation in any material way from other Israelites. True, they have no past, no genealogy except that accorded to them by Abraham and Sarah. But they have the same future as everyone in holy Israel: a portion in the world to come. Obliterating boundaries of history and genealogy, race and language and territory, tearing down the walls that in this-worldly terms separate humanity, overcoming difference by appeal to transcendence, the Torah imparts the vision of how God sees us, instead of how we see ourselves. That is the difference between a religion that aspires to serve God and an ethnic religion, through which we serve ourselves. By the normative Judaism, which is to say, the Torah of our sages of blessed memory, the children of the flesh are the children of the promise. In the Torah, God has defined Israel. All the rest is commentary; it is our task then to go and study—and bring to fulfillment the lessons that we learn.

God has called us as messengers to humanity, and the Torah is our message.

What Is at Stake
in the Sanctity of Israel?

WHAT HAPPENS WHEN the messenger forgets the message? Our sages expressed their theology through a myth of genealogy. Today, the myth is no longer grasped; all that survives of theological genealogy is the now-failing taboo against intermarriage, lacking all reasoned explanation. The unearned grace of the ancestors bringing blessing to their offspring—*zekhut avot,* the merit of the patriarchs and matriarchs, a deeply intangible conception of the continuity of generations in the faith—gives way to a quite material and ordinary conviction that the group must endure despite it all. But spite is not a reason. No wonder then that the God whom sages met in the Torah falls silent to heirs who know that they are special but have forgotten why.

To show what this means in the world of here and now, let me tell two stories out of my own meeting with frail Jewish life in Nordic Europe. Here is where I found an urgent and compelling need to write this book: I could not desist.

The first story takes place in Åbo (in Suomi/Finnish: Turku). There I went to Sabbath services on the first Sabbath of my term as Visiting Research Professor at Åbo Akademi's Research Institute, just after Passover. The Jewish community in Åbo, Finland's second largest city, numbers about a hundred fifty; perhaps twenty came to synagogue worship despite snow that morning, a remarkable turn-out, I thought. I had second thoughts, however, when I found that while the congregation assembled for Sabbath worship to hear the Torah declaimed, as it is Mondays, Thursdays, and Sabbaths in every synagogue across the world, in Åbo that morning they had decided to omit the weekly lection. It was not because the synagogue was Reform or had any doctrinal objections to hearing the Torah declaimed. It was, to the contrary, an Orthodox synagogue, signified by separate seating for women and men. It was because the people did not think reading the Torah was important, so they dropped it that day.

No one explained why. I was supposed to understand what was not going to happen. The ark was never opened. The Torah was never removed, unclad, opened, proclaimed in mighty song, as it was that Sabbath everywhere else in the world of holy Israel. Here, in a synagogue of Orthodox Jews (most of them of Lithuanian origin, native Finns, three or four generations in Turku), men and women had come to the synagogue on the Sabbath out of a deep sense of Jewish loyalty but omitted from their worship the reason that Judaism specifies for coming to the synagogue at all. I was asked to speak, and I pointed out to them that, on the Sabbath following Passover, the only synagogue in the world, from Reconstructionist to Orthodox, Reform to Hasidic, that omitted opening the Torah and declaiming its contents to assembled Israel was the one I had stumbled on in Turku.

The Talmud is explicit that people may say their prayers at home, not in a quorum, except for the requirement of hearing the Torah declaimed; for that, they must come to the synagogue (or form a quorum of their own, which is the same thing). When we say our prayers, we speak to God; when the Torah is read, God speaks to us, holy Israel—that is, Jews made holy by the sanctifying act of accepting the Torah. All of this was lost in Åbo, by people who really just wanted to get together and run through the old words in the old way, rehearsing what is familiar, without much inconvenience.

When I spoke, I said that I'd visited synagogues throughout the world and had learned something new in every one of them. But here I learned what I did not know was there to be learned: there is in this world an Orthodox synagogue that assembles for Shabbat worship and leaves the Torah orphaned in its ark. Not having a rabbi, the lay people perhaps thought that wrong was right. But the simple fact is, we are Israel, holy Israel, by reason of the Torah, and without the Torah, we have no reason to come into being at all. If the community's two Torah readers were fatigued because Passover had just ended (as I was told), then it was time for others to learn what it takes to do the work properly. British Orthodox Judaism has recognized the problem in small communities and has advised reading the Torah not in the received, ancient chant and from a scroll in Hebrew without vowels, which takes much work in preparation, but from a book, even in English. The content is what matters most of all. But here I met Orthodoxy without Torah: a Jewish community without pride and self-respect, I concluded, had sustained itself over time, even while giving Judaism—the Torah—an indecent burial. The least we owe ourselves is to honor our reason for being.

Then came a still more striking discovery. In Stockholm, later that spring, I found myself involved in a controversy and for the first time in my life realized the full weight and meaning of the secularization of Israel. I learned what I had never fully perceived at home in the United States, which is, what it means when Jews lose all contact with Judaism, the Torah. To explain briefly: a professor of the history of religion at Uppsala University, Jan Bergman (whom I had known for nearly a quarter century), from the late 1980s had made a series of scandalous and ignorant anti-Semitic statements about Judaism. As a result, scholars of Judaism throughout the world protested against an anti-Semite teaching about Judaism as part of the Uppsala University theological faculty. I participated, with articles in the *National Jewish Post* and with the *Encyclopaedia Britannica Yearbook* article on Judaism, which I wrote for some decades. When I reached Åbo, I found in the mail a document from Bergman, in which he clearly indicated that he did not regard himself as an anti-Semite, did not wish to espouse anti-Semitic opinions, and wanted to retract and apologize for statements of an anti-Semitic, anti-Judaic, anti-Zionist, and Holocaust-revisionist character that he had made or that had been imputed to him.

Now, in Åbo, I read his document—in my elementary Swedish it took work—and was reminded of how, in the late 1920s, Henry Ford had apologized for the anti-Semitic character of his *Dearborn Independent* and how, from that time onward, the anti-Semitic character of the boardrooms of American industry was called into question and ultimately (a long time later) delegitimized. It struck me that if Bergman's apology and retraction were to take place, anti-Semitism, anti-Judaism, anti-Zionism, and Holocaust revisionism would lose legitimacy in the academic world. Here a university figure would find himself compelled to acknowledge the honor of Israel, the Jewish people; the legitimacy and vitality of Judaism, the religion; the facticity of the Holocaust; and the right of the state of Israel to a secure, permanent, and honorable position among the nations of the world. Such a statement would begin that process of the academic delegitimation of anti-Semitism and its companions.

When I went to Stockholm in early June, I met with the leaders of the Stockholm Committee Against Anti-Semitism and the president of the Stockholm Jewish Community, and securing from them a list of complaints against Bergman, I met with Bergman himself. He drew up a response to every item, apologizing for some, denying that he had said others, and repudiating statements made in his name by third parties. At every point he took a position of genuine regret for what he had said and done and undertook never to repeat these actions and statements that had so disgraced his name.

When I returned to Åbo, I found letters from the Committee Against Anti-Semitism and the president of the Stockholm Jewish Community making it clear that they rejected any possibility of a reconciliation with Bergman based on Bergman's retraction and apology. I made it clear that Judaism makes provision for the penitence of a sinner, and they denied all possibility that Bergman was ever going to be able to right his relationship with the Jewish community and with Judaism. When I introduced the concept of *teshuvah*, repentance—which is a critical moral category of the theology of Judaism—and pointed out that, on the day of atonement, we ask God to forgive us our sins, I found complete incomprehension, indeed, what I regarded as an attitude of disrespect. Here, for the first time in my life, I came face to face with the results of the total secularization of the Jews: their incapacity to respond to the most compelling and insistent teachings of the Torah (that is, of Judaism), their absolute refusal to behave in a concrete circumstance in accord with the morality of *teshuvah*, which forms the foundation of our relationship with God.

I determined to face the issue head-on, and I wrote a letter to Stockholm's Committee Against Anti-Semitism that frames issues of morality in the setting of the theology of Judaism. Here is the Judaic theological position in contrast to the secular ethnic one, the possibility of forgiveness in the model of God the all-merciful, as against the attitude of unending ethnic retaliation for unforgivable hurt. My message to Stockholm's Committee Against Anti-Semitism concludes my case. The Committee Against Anti-Semitism did not respond:

> Shall the affairs of Judaism, the religion, and the Jewish community (Hebrew: *am yisrael*) be conducted in accord with the Torah, revealed by God to Moses at Mount Sinai, or in accord with a secular principle defined, ad hoc, by whom it may concern? That is what is at stake in the matter at hand, and I shall try to explain to you what is at stake.
>
> You clearly do not grasp the facts or the issues at hand, which I set forth here for all concerned. Permit me to instruct you about the religion, Judaism, which governs the attitudes and actions of the faithful in this dispute, and, indeed, in the conduct of the public policy of the Jewish community, so far as that community realizes the religion, Judaism, or, in the native category of Judaism, the Torah. For we are Jews by reason of Judaism, meaning, we frame our actions and faith in response to the commandments of God in the Torah. If you do not share our premises, you of course are free to frame matters by appeal to a different religion or to some secular code, but then you may no longer claim the moral authority of the Torah that, from the perspective of God, defines us as holy Israel. I undertake to instruct you in these matters, since, it is clear to me, you do not grasp what is at stake in the proper conduct of a dispute, including the resolution of this particular dispute, which is now at hand. As a result, you write in a captious and, as I shall explain in detail, disrespectful manner, which is therefore un-Judaic and contrary to the teachings of the Torah.
>
> Anti-Semitism, anti-Judaism, anti-Zionism, Holocaust revisionism, in all forms, inclusive of systematic delegitimization of the right of the state of Israel to a secure existence, are public issues, not mediated by any committee. In the case of Professor Bergman, they also are academic issues, since the focus of protest has been his position at Uppsala University and his (mis)represen-

tation of Judaism in that professorship. On that basis was solicited the active involvement of the entire academic world, and on that basis, I took part in the protests from the very start, and in public, and in the press. Many others did too.

The religion, Judaism, rests on the principal commandment, "You shall not bear a grudge nor pursue a dispute beyond reason, nor hate your brother in your heart, but you shall love your neighbor as yourself" (Lev. 19:18). What that means is, it is a religious duty to turn an enemy into a friend, if that is possible. The basis within Judaism for the resolution of disputes, within the commandment of God to Moses in the Torah just now cited, is in the halakhah of *teshuvah,* which occurs in the authoritative legal statements of Judaism and which is summarized in Maimonides' Hilkhot Teshuvah. To understand the Judaic way of conducting a dispute, however bitter, you must inform yourselves at the very least of the theology and law that governs, with or without the sanction of the Jewish community of Stockholm, by reason of God's commandment. That is what defines public policy in the community of Judaism. If you do not accept these premises, then, of course, no discourse is possible; you will not grasp the actions of those of us who do, and we have no way of communicating with you. The Jewish community—meaning, in Hebrew, *am yisrael*—is in this context not a political entity but a religious body, called into being by God at Sinai through the covenant of the Torah. That is what is always at stake in the public life of Judaism, and that is what governs here.

On that basis, as an action of religious conviction, I both participated in the worldwide expressions of protest against Professor Bergman's anti-Semitic, anti-Judaic, anti-Israel, and Holocaust-revisionist statements, but also took note, in the long documentation that ensued, of his insistence that he did not say this, did not mean that, had been misquoted there, and so on and so forth. What this signaled was that, despite public statements and actions to the contrary, he did not wish to be regarded and was not in his intention anti-Semitic, anti-Judaic, and so on. While the intention does not change the fact, it does recast the situation. What it meant to me, in reading his statements, was, and is, that he wished to retract statements he made that were in fact anti-Semitic, anti-Judaic, and the like, and apologize for them; that he wished to repudiate statements made in his name by others; that he wished to condemn the way in which statements of his have been used, and the like. I read all of this to indicate that he wished to achieve a reconciliation with the Jewish community (meaning, once more, in Hebrew, *am yisrael* in the theological sense explained above). I saw the possibility of achieving such a reconciliation. In my view, only good could come of what has now come about. Once one party to the dispute wishes to express apology, retraction, and ask for forgiveness, as Mishnah Yoma 9:8 says in so many words, the aggrieved party has the religious obligation to respond appropriately. The Jewish community (*am yisrael*) has no alternative, within Judaism, but to make possible the act of true reconciliation, involving specification of what has been done wrong, for which the offending party explicitly apologizes, and a statement of regret and resolve not to repeat those wrongs. These are matters that are spelled out in the Mishnah, which, beyond the written Torah, is the first document of the oral Torah and authoritative. I suggest you consult the passage and compare its contents with my account of them. In my judgment Professor Bergman's statement meets the definition just now given.

You cannot defend Judaism if you do not honor the religion yourself and fulfill its requirements as these pertain in context. Each person speaks out of the moral authority, learning, and public record that he or she has written over a lifetime. No one has alleged that you "sanctioned" anyone else's engagement, since no one has asked you for such a "sanction." This is a public issue, and all engaged parties have the right to pursue it in a public way; there are no monopolies when it comes to anti-Judaism, anti-Semitism, anti-Zionism, Holocaust revisionism, and other issues critical to the existence of the Jewish community (transcending the Jewish Community of Stockholm). Your letter to me does not suggest you understand that simple fact. That you "sanctioned" no such meeting is therefore irrelevant to the state of the question. No one thought, or said, you did. That you expressed views on the issues, which I recorded and reviewed with you, is the fact. That Professor Bergman's statement does not conclude matters from your perspective certainly is a position you have a right to take, and no one will argue with you about that fact. Nor does anyone doubt you will express yourselves in print in the future as in the past. That is right and proper; everyone will exercise that right.

Bergman has now repented (to use the Judaic theological category) or apologized for the statements he made and repudiated statements imputed to him that he did not make (to use more secular language). This was a *mahloqet leshem shamayim,* a dispute for the sake of Heaven, which is to say, for the honor that we owe to God; but once the action of apology and regret has been offered, by the law of Judaism that governs all of holy Israel, to pursue the matter is no longer a *mahloqet leshem shamayim.*

In my opening paragraphs I specified the source of authority over faithful Israel; now, therefore, appeal to me by reference to the Torah, and I shall listen. Appeal to me by reason of the petty politics of a perfectly secular world, and, for the record, I shall not respond. We are all free and responsible, and our responsibility is to God and the Torah, which are remarkable for their absence from any and all of your communications. It is an act of responsibility on my part to take the trouble to explain matters of the Torah's commandments, which do obligate us all, to you. To state the point in as simple and clear language as I can: in Judaism, which is at stake here and always, there is only a religious basis for reconciliation, and many of us do live out our lives, to the best of our abilities, within the Torah. Without that basis, there is no right or wrong, good or evil, let alone moral authority that compels assent and action.

To conclude: the theology of *teshuvah* in the context of the written Torah, the oral Torah, and the codes, in Maimonides' formulation of it as normative law, makes provision for the resolution of long-term conflict. Your memo is written in a spirit that contradicts the halakhah of *teshuvah,* and you place yourselves in danger of losing the moral authority that, until this point, has lent weight to your righteous protests against Professor Bergman's anti-Semitic, anti-Judaic statements; moral authority has sustained you, among us all as the Jewish community (Hebrew: *am yisrael*); it is all that we have—or should aspire to. It is now your task to inform yourselves on whether or not I have accurately represented the religion, Judaism, and, if I have, to conform to that religion if you presume to represent it. As a rabbi, I instruct you to do so.

Here is how I frame what is at stake in my insistence that Israel can represent only that holy Israel that stands every day at Sinai and in word and in deed every day proclaims, "We shall do and we shall hear." So we respond to God, when God says to us, "You shall be holy, as I the Lord your God am holy."

Notes

Preface

1. "Israel" in these pages always refers to the Jewish people, the people of Israel, of the liturgy and holy books of Judaism. All other uses of "Israel" are qualified, e.g., Land of Israel, God of Israel, State of Israel. Note 3 expands on this point.

2. That is the burden of my *A Rabbi Talks with Jesus: An Intermillennial, Interfaith Exchange* (New York: Doubleday, 1993), to which this book forms a sequel. I see a "Judaism" as comprising a way of life, a worldview, and a definition of the social entity ("Israel") that follows the one and embodies the other. A natural sequel to the present work will address the matter of "worldview," the third element in the tripartite composition of a Judaism. For the counterpart Judaisms spelled out in the rabbinic literature that has set the norms for Judaism from antiquity to the present day, see my *The Transformation of Judaism: From Philosophy to Religion* (Champaign, Ill.: University of Illinois Press, 1992). There I spell out two Judaisms, closely related but clearly differentiated, the one set forth by the Mishnah and related writings, the other by the first of the two Talmuds and its associated documents, the former philosophical in classification, the latter, religious (in terms defined there).

3. I am speaking of the "Israel" of the religion, Judaism, which is to say, the "Israel" of which the Hebrew Scriptures ("Old Testament") are believed by Judaism to speak. That is that "Israel after the flesh" that is also the "Israel after the spirit" of Judaism: the holy people, Israel. In today's world the word "Israel" commonly is made to refer to the State of Israel, and the word "Israeli" to a citizen of that nation. "Israel" also may refer to a particular place, namely, the State of Israel or the Land of Israel. But that

narrow and particularly political and geographic meaning is new, beginning, as it does, in 1948. Long prior to that time, and even today, there has
been a second and distinct meaning, "Israel" as "all Jews everywhere," the
people of Israel. This "Israel" defined as "the Jewish people," sometimes
spelled with a capital P as "the Jewish People," identifies "Israel" with a
trans-national "community." It is a very important meaning of the word,
for Scripture's many references to "Israel," as in "the Guardian of Israel
does not slumber or sleep," then are taken to refer to that people or People.
Throughout the liturgy of the synagogue, "Israel" always refers to the
people, wherever they live, and not to the State of Israel today. The fact that
these two meanings, the one particular to a state, the other general to a
scattered group, contradict one another alerts us to a problem. It is that a
single word may stand for two things. Here, the political "Israel" meaning
the State of Israel and the religious "Israel" meaning the holy people of
God, the children of Israel of which Scripture speaks, are not to be confused
but to be kept apart. I speak here only of holy Israel and the religion,
Judaism, that defines that Israel. All discussions of Judaism as an ethnic
religion in this book concern Judaism as formulated in the diaspora or
"Golah" (Exile). The representation of that same Judaism in the State of
Israel takes place in a political and social setting so utterly different from
that of the diaspora that a quite separate discussion of ethnicity and religion
is required—if the category, "ethnic," applies at all. As I state in so many
words in Chapter Five, how things are to be sorted out in that other,
political and geographic context of Judaism, I do not claim to know. The
theoretical literature on the study of Judaism in the State of Israel is in
its elementary stages, and the phenomena that it describes, analyzes, and
interprets themselves are only in their beginning stages as well, the state
being not fifty years old. By contrast, the diaspora-Judaism that people
broadly know has existed in its present form for well over a century and
perhaps, in some places, as long as two centuries. It goes without saying, too, that the formulation of the issue in the context of Christianity
is natural to the diaspora but not to the State of Israel, where Judaism's
conversation-partner—if there is one—must be Islam. So this is a work
of the Exile (as Israelis have it). And, it hardly needs adding in light of
chapter 5, it also is a work of the America and the Judaism that this writer
professes as citizenship, nationality, on the one side, and religion, on the
other.

   4. James D. G. Dunn's *The Partings of the Ways Between Christianity
and Judaism and Their Significance for the Character of Christianity* (Philadelphia: Trinity Press International, 1991).

   5. That is the argument of my *Telling Tales: Making Sense of Christian*

and Judaic Nonsense—The Urgency and Basis for Judaeo-Christian Dialogue (Louisville: Westminster-John Knox Press, 1993).

Chapter 1

1. (Philadelphia: Trinity Press International, 1991.) In focusing on Dunn's formulation of the definition of *Judaism* and on his explanation of why Christianity and (that) Judaism parted company, I do not mean to neglect numerous other important works. For example, two books by my colleague and friend Professor Heikki Räisänen of the University of Helsinki frame matters in quite different ways: *Paul and the Law* (Tübingen: J. C. B. Mohr, 1983); and *The Torah and Christ: Essays in German and English on the Problem of the Law in Early Christianity* (Helsinki: Suomen Eksegeettisen Seuran Julkaisuja/Finnish Exegetical Society, 1986). I have found his book and essays stimulating and rich. But the particular concern of this book, the allegation that Judaism is an ethnic religion, does not require that we consider the role of the Torah or the law in the relationship between Judaism and Christianity; indeed, that issue is extrinsic to the question of ethnicity in Dunn's formulation. And more to the point, this book is not an essay on the study of Paul but an exercise in the analysis of terms critical to rabbinic Judaism's conception of Israel.

The question of how various ancient authors, Judaic or Jewish or gentile, distinguished between the ethnic and the holy Israel is not taken up here, nor do we consider data on how the Roman government regarded the Jews. These matters have no bearing on the theological problem treated in this book. For a valuable piece of information on Roman imperial distinction between the ethnic and the religious Israel, see Martin Goldman, "Nerva, the Fiscus Judaicus, and Jewish Identity," *Journal of Roman Studies* 79 (1989): 40–44. A history of views of Israel as an ethnic group, inclusive of how Ezra's legislation squares with the (later) conception that through conversion, not ethnic-territorial assimilation, people might enter Israel, awaits its author.

2. Not all Christian theories of Israel treat Israel as ethnic; Joseph Cardinal Ratzinger invokes the language of "mystery" and "eternity," and Paul van Buren's theology of Israel introduces issues of sanctification and transcendence. But Dunn certainly represents the broadest range of Christian opinion.

3. James D. G. Dunn, *The Partings of the Ways Between Christianity and Judaism and Their Significance for the Character of Christianity* (Philadelphia: Trinity Press International, 1991), 230.

4. Ibid., 258–59.

5. Jonathan Z. Smith, "Fences and Neighbors," in W. S. Green, ed., *Approaches to Ancient Judaism* (Missoula, Mont.: Scholars Press for Brown Judaic Studies, 1978), 2:1–25; and Smith, *Imagining Religion: From Babylon to Jonestown* (Chicago: University of Chicago Press, 1982), 1–18.

6. Smith, "Fences and Neighbors."

7. Obviously, I do not intend to enter into a single question of Pauline exegesis. A fine introduction to the contemporary state of a variety of critical issues relevant here is in Terence L. Donaldson, "'Riches for the Gentiles' (Rom. 11:12): Israel's Rejection and Paul's Gentile Mission," *Journal of Biblical Literature* 112 (1993): 81–98. I have read with real appreciation many of the current books on Paul and Judaism; so far as I have observed, none calls into question the observation offered here, that Paul distinguishes the ethnic from the religious. That is the main point required for the argument at hand.

8. I owe these points to Rev. Dr. William H. Scarle, Jr., pastor of Franklin Union Baptist Church, Worthington, Pennsylvania., from his letter of June 11, 1993.

Chapter 2

1. Dunn, *The Parting of the Ways Between Christianity and Judaism and Their Significance for the Character of Christianity* (Philadelphia: Trinity Press International, 1991), 8.

2. I have argued that the formation of the conception of Israel and Roman as counterparts first surfaces in the documents framed after Christianity became the religion of the Roman Empire, in my *Judaism and Christianity in the Age of Constantine: Issues of the Initial Confrontation* (Chicago: University of Chicago Press, 1987).

3. See Robin Scroggs, *The Last Adam: A Study in Pauline Anthropology* (Philadelphia: Fortress Press, 1966).

4. In my *Messiah in Context: Israel's History and Destiny in Formative Judaism* (Philadelphia: Fortress Press, 1984) I found that, in the Mishnaic stratum, the Messiah theme also functioned as a mode of hierarchical classification. Interestingly, classified by *Messiah* was a kind of priest; hence as in the present case, the hierarchical issue proved one of caste. So the matters are systemically uniform.

Chapter 3

1. This is spelled out in my *Judaism and Christianity in the Age of Constantine: Issues of the Initial Confrontation* (Chicago: University of Chicago Press, 1987).

2. I have spelled out the conception of paradigm as it applies to Scripture's account of Israel and its history in my *The Presence of the Past, the Pastness of the Present: History, Time, and Paradigm in Rabbinic Judaism* (Bethesda, Md.: CDL Press, 1995).

3. As I have already pointed out, converts did not present an anomaly, of course, since they were held to be children of Abraham and Sarah, who had "made souls," that is, converts, in Haran, a point repeated in the documents of the period.

Chapter 4

1. Today we have to add "of one religion or no other religion than Judaism"; thus, "the Jews are a people of one religion or none." I am confident that this formulation accords with the nearly universal consensus of the Judaic faithful and of nearly all Jews by ethnic affiliation. The conception of "Jews for Jesus," or "Messianic Jews," has found remarkably slight assent within ethnic Israel in the diaspora. For the purposes of the state of Israel's law of return or citizenship law, matters have to be defined as well; that is not relevant to this book's discussion.

2. This is the argument of my *Judaism and Christianity in the Age of Constantine: Issues of the Initial Confrontation* (Chicago: University of Chicago Press, 1987).

3. Eusebius, "The Proof of the Gospel," in Colm Luibheid, *The Essential Eusebius* (New York: Mentor, 1966).

4. Adolph Harnack, *The Mission and Expansion of Christianity in the First Three Centuries* (London, 1908; reprinted by Peter Smith, Gloucester, 1972), 256–57.

Chapter 5

1. This formulation of matters echoes the argument of my *Judaism's Theological Voice: The Melody of the Talmud* (Chicago: University of Chicago Press, 1995).

2. The state of Israel represents a quite different set of problems awaiting analysis in its own terms and context.

Bibliography

Donaldson, Terence L. "'Riches for the Gentiles' (Rom. 11:12): Israel's Rejection and Paul's Gentile Mission." *Journal of Biblical Literature* 112 (1993): 81–98.

Dunn, James D. G. *The Partings of the Ways Between Christianity and Judaism and Their Significance for the Character of Christianity.* Philadelphia: Trinity Press International, 1991.

Gärtner, B. *The Temple and the Community in Qumran and the New Testament.* Cambridge, U.K.: Cambridge University Press, 1965.

Goodenough, Erwin R. *By Light, Light: The Mystic Gospel of Hellenistic Judaism.* New Haven, Conn.: Yale University Press, 1935.

Goodman, Martin. "Nerva, the Fiscus Judaicus, and Jewish Identity." *Journal of Roman Studies* 79 (1989): 40–44.

Harnack, Adolph. *The Mission and Expansion of Christianity in the First Three Centuries.* London, 1908; reprinted by Peter Smith, Gloucester, 1972.

Neusner, Jacob. *Aphrahat and Judaism: The Christian Jewish Argument in Fourth Century Iran.* Leiden: Brill, 1971.

———. *Jews and Christians: The Myth of a Common Tradition.* New York: Trinity Press International, 1990.

———. *Judaism and Christianity in the Age of Constantine: Issues of the Initial Confrontation.* Chicago: University of Chicago Press, 1987.

———. *Judaism and Its Social Metaphors: Israel in the History of Jewish Thought.* New York: Cambridge University Press, 1988.

———. *Judaism in the Beginning of Christianity.* Philadelphia: Fortress Press, 1983.

———. *Judaism in the Matrix of Christianity.* Philadelphia: Fortress Press, 1986.

————. *Judaism's Theological Voice: The Melody of the Talmud.* Chicago: University of Chicago Press, 1995.

————. *Judaism Without Christianity: An Introduction to the Religious System of the Mishnah in Historical Context.* Hoboken, N.J.: Ktav Publishing House, 1991.

————. *Messiah in Context: Israel's History and Destiny in Formative Judaism.* Philadelphia: Fortress Press, 1984.

————. *The Presence of the Past, The Pastness of the Present: History, Time, and Paradigm in Rabbinic Judaism.* Bethesda, Md.: CDL Press, 1995.

————. *A Rabbi Talks with Jesus: An Intermillennial, Interfaith Exchange.* New York: Doubleday, 1993.

————. *Telling Tales: Making Sense of Christian and Judaic Nonsense— The Urgency and Basis for Judaeo-Christian Dialogue.* Louisville: Westminster-John Knox Press, 1993.

————. *"To See Ourselves as Others See Us": Jews, Christians, "Others" in Late Antiquity.* Chico, Calif.: Scholars Press, 1985.

————. *The Transformation of Judaism: From Philosophy to Religion.* Champaign: University of Illinois Press, 1992.

————, ed. *The Christian and Judaic Invention of History.* Studies in Religion Series. Atlanta: Scholars Press for American Academy of Religion, 1990.

————, ed. *Judaism in Cold War America: 1945–1990.* Vol. 4, *Judaism and Christianity: The New Relationship.* New York: Garland Press, 1991.

Neusner, Jacob, and Bruce D. Chilton. *Christianity and Judaism: The Formative Categories.* Vol. 1, *Revelation: The Torah and the Bible.* Philadelphia: Trinity Press International, 1995.

————. *Christianity and Judaism: The Formative Categories.* Vol. 2, *The Body of Faith: Israel and Church.* Philadelphia: Trinity Press International, 1995.

————. *Christianity and Judaism: The Formative Categories.* Vol. 3, *God in the World.* Philadelphia: Trinity Press International, 1995.

————. *Judaeo-Christian Debates: Communion with God, the Kingdom of God, the Mystery of the Messiah.* Minneapolis: Fortress Press, 1995.

Neusner, Jacob, and Andrew M. Greeley. *The Bible and Us: A Priest and a Rabbi Read the Scriptures Together.* New York: Warner Books, 1990.

Neusner, Jacob, and William Scott Green, eds. *Judaisms and Their Messiahs in the Beginning of Christianity.* New York: Cambridge University Press, 1987.

————. eds. *The Origins of Judaism: Religion, History, and Literature in*

Late Antiquity. Vols. 6 and 7, *Judaism and Christianity in the First Century.* New York: Garland Press, 1991.

Räisänen, Heikki. *Paul and the Law.* Tübingen: J. C. B. Mohr, 1983.

———. *The Torah and Christ: Essays in German and English on the Problem of the Law in Early Christianity.* Helsinki: Suomen Eksegeettisen Seuran Julkaisuja/Finnish Exegetical Society, 1986.

Sandelin, Karl-Gustav. *Wisdom as Nourisher: A Study of an Old Testament Theme, Its Development Within Early Judaism, and Its Impact on Early Christianity.* Åbo: Åbo Akademi, 1986.

Scroggs, Robin. *The Last Adam: A Study in Pauline Anthropology.* Philadelphia: Fortress Press, 1966.

Smith, Jonathan Z. "Fences and Neighbors." In *Approaches to Ancient Judaism,* edited by W. S. Green. Missoula, Mont.: Scholars Press for Brown Judaic Studies, 1978.

———. *Imaging Religion: From Babylon to Jonestown.* Chicago: University of Chicago Press, 1982.

Vermes, Geza. *The Dead Sea Scrolls in English.* 2d ed. Harmondsworth, U.K.: Penguin, 1975.

———. *The Dead Sea Scrolls: Qumran in Perspective.* London: Collins, 1977.

Wolfson, Harry Austryn. *Philo: Foundations of Religious Philosophy in Judaism, Christianity, and Islam.* Cambridge, Mass.: Harvard University Press, 1948.

Index